That's Not What I Meant!

That's Not What I Meant!

TIM STAFFORD

ZondervanPublishingHouse
Grand Rapids, Michigan

A Division of HarperCollinsPublishers

That's Not What I Meant!
Copyright © 1995 Tim Stafford

Requests for information should be addressed to:
   Zondervan Publishing House
   Grand Rapids, MI 49530

ISBN 0-310-49001-4

Edited by John Sloan

Printed in the United States of America

Contents

Introduction:
Pictures of the Power of Words

May the words of my mouth and the meditation of my heart be pleasing in your sight, O Lord, my Rock and my Redeemer.

(Psalm 19:14)

My mother was a great knitter. She never went to meetings without her ball of yarn and a sweater-in-progress. At home she was forever holding up sections of a new work against my arms or chest or back, to see whether it would fit. Unfortunately, not all of her sweaters were triumphs. Often the size or shape or color was decidedly odd.

I do remember one outstanding success, however. When I was in the seventh grade, she produced a bright red cable knit sweater, very distinctive and attractive. I got it for Christmas and proudly wore it to school, where a boy noticed it and looked it over critically.

"It looks like a girl's sweater," he said.

I never wore the sweater out of the house again.

∾∘∾

A quiet, introspective girl—let's call her Martha—attended a large public high school outside Indianapolis. Martha's shyness kept her from having very many friends. She got to her senior year in high school without ever having a date.

That fall a very popular girl, Julie, was assigned as her lab partner in chemistry. Julie thought Martha was nice, and invited her to a Halloween party. It was, Martha told her mother, her first party invitation since she was eight years old.

Martha was scared to death when she walked in the door of Julie's home. She said hello to the people she knew, she drank a Coke, she listened in on several group conversations. In one corner of the living room was a group of boys, laughing uproariously. They would look around the room, talk in low voices, then laugh. At one point Martha glanced over at them and saw that the whole group was looking straight at her. They burst into hilarious laughter, covering their mouths, doubling over. Martha looked the other way, blushing hard.

Later in the evening a boy she knew slightly sat down next to her on the sofa and asked how she knew Julie. They talked about school for a while, about teachers they had in common. Then Martha remembered that this boy, Rich, had been in the group that was laughing. She asked him what it had been about.

Rich colored slightly, hesitated, then told her that they had been playing a game where you look at people and try to say what animal they look like.

"Oh," she said. "Like did you do Julie? What animal was she?"

"Julie is easy," he said. "A deer." Which did seem right to Martha—those large, brown eyes.

"Mark is a giraffe," Rich said. "Cheryl is a chipmunk."

He went on to tell her what animal five or six people had been paired with."

"What about me?" Martha said, her heart in her throat.

"You did me. I saw you."

"Sure," he said. For a moment he paused. "You're a dog." And he couldn't help cracking up a little bit all over again.

When Martha got home that night, she looked in the mirror and saw, sure enough, just what he had said: a dog. A cocker spaniel, to be precise. Her blond-brown hair hanging down on each side, like a cocker's ears. Her chinless mouth. She was mortified. For many years afterward she remained acutely self-conscious whenever she thought boys were looking at her. Often when she looked at herself in the mirror, she thought to herself, "You're a dog."

~∞~

Rob was laid off from his job in September. With three children to support and with house payments, he was soon in a panic. Sometimes he sat in the kitchen the whole day, afraid to go out and face the world.

When he had been out of work a month, his church got wind of his troubles and started providing meals. After three weeks, Ted dropped off a spaghetti dinner and sat awhile, talking with Rob about his situation. Then, after a pause, Ted cleared his throat.

"This may sound strange," he said, "because I know from your angle it's hard to see how you're going to get through this. But I am quite sure that you are going to get a job, probably a good job. I don't know when and I don't know where. But I know you are a good, hard worker, the kind of guy people want to hire. I know you are looking hard for work. And I know that God loves you and will take care of you.

Someday you're going to be looking back on this time, and you'll be able to see as clear as daylight that God was watching over you."

Rob wasn't all that moved at the time, but the words stuck with him. He knew Ted meant what he said, and that Ted was no fool. Ted's encouragement made a subtle but substantial difference in Rob's attitude. The feeling of panic dissipated. He figured Ted was probably right: he would get a job if he kept looking. Which, in fact, is exactly what happened.

He often thought of Ted's words in later years when other friends of his were going through hard times, or when his own kids graduated from school and were looking for work. A few times, when he felt it was appropriate, he passed on a version of Ted's encouragement.

Actually, Ted's words—backed by his character—made quite a difference in Rob's life. They helped him through a difficult passage, and more basically, they helped him develop a different, more fundamentally optimistic view of hard times. Though he went through other distressing periods in his life, he was never again so scared.

∾∘∾

When my wife Popie was in the sixth grade, she was a member of the popular crowd. Every Friday night she and her friends gathered at the country club to drink Pepsis and do the twist. Popie led the list of girls to be called before school to see what everyone was wearing.

One day her teacher asked her to stay after school. When they were alone she asked Popie if she had ever heard of India's caste system. Popie said no, so her teacher explained it to her. She drew a little sketch on the blackboard, explaining that a Brahmin, in the top caste, could not even allow an Untouchable's shadow to fall on him.

"You and your friends," the teacher said thoughtfully, "remind me of those Brahmins."

Popie did not cry. She did not even let the teacher know how those words affected her. But they did, deeply. She was shocked. She had never realized the ugly meaning of the word "exclusive." She had never thought about the way she and her friends affected those who didn't belong to the popular crowd.

Strange to say, that brief conversation changed Popie's life. She became one of the most *inclusive* persons I have ever met. Thirty years later Popie could remember her teacher's words as though they were spoken yesterday.

⟿◦⟿

Mark and Robin married when they were both in their thirties. It was his first marriage, her second. Their conflicts began over work schedules. Mark was used to working long hours. His work also required travel. Robin, however, often felt neglected. She told Mark once that he should have married his work instead of her. Mark tried to be reasonable, but he had a hard time taking her complaints seriously.

At Robin's insistence they went to a marriage counselor. It was in the counselor's office that they had their worst fight ever. Robin actually screamed at Mark. It was all he could do to stay calm and not yell back.

Then, near the end of the session, the counselor asked Robin what she wanted to do. Did she want to continue with more counseling?

"I want a divorce!" Robin said.

Until then Mark had thought he was having a stressful

quarrel with his wife. But with that one word, autumn changed to winter. Mark didn't want a divorce. Robin said, the next day, that she didn't either. But Mark could never wholly put aside that moment of revelation, when he had seen that she did not hold their marriage sacred. She was willing to toss him aside, he thought, just like her first husband. He couldn't shake that thought. Mark became more self-protective, less willing to give in. He began to consciously look out for his own interests.

They were divorced about a year later.

They had their problems, and it would have been hard to mend them. They needed help. Instead they got gutted by a word used carelessly: "divorce."

⚭

Words are very powerful. Many people, if they take time, can think of wise words from a teacher, a parent, or a friend that made a great impact on their direction in life. Many people can spotlight an encouraging word that lifted them at a very low time. Many people can also remember some searing knife of a word, the memory of which brings blushing shame even today, years later.

Words can hurt. Words can heal. Therefore it is of the utmost importance that we pay attention to our words—not merely the words we intend but also those that slip out when we are not paying attention.

CHAPTER ONE

Outside In:
A Way to Change Your Life

From the fruit of his lips a man is filled with good things,
as surely as the work of his hands rewards him.

(Proverbs 12:14)

Our words matter. The book of Genesis portrays God's creating the world by speaking. In a related way we humans create the world we live in through our words. The way we talk to each other makes a world full of love and security, or a world of bitterness and anxiety.

Take a married couple. The man doesn't talk. To compensate, his wife talks too much. In particular, she shoots off her mouth about his mother. If you press him, he would admit that his mother is far from perfect. But he simply doesn't want to hear it all the time, even (especially?) from his wife. To him, the running down of his mother is like a dripping faucet. It's not any particular drip that kills him; it's the wearing effect of the whole thing.

Of course, he doesn't tell his wife this. He knows that would just start a fight, and he doesn't want to get into that. He figures he can hunker down and live with her complaints. But they wear on him.

What wears on his wife is his silence. She wants to hear that her husband loves her, and likes the way she looks. He does compliment her cooking, but that doesn't help. She knows she is a good cook. Her attractiveness is what she needs affirmed.

Her husband is not a sentimental person, and she knew that when she married him. She *didn't* know how wearisome it would be. She is tired of taking the initiative; she wants *him* to bring a little romance to the marriage. For a long time she tried to wheedle it out of him, but she's given that up. He just won't listen to her needs, she says.

Can anyone help these two? A moralistic approach won't work; they both can give you nine yards of reasons why they're justified in their behavior. Anyway, neither one is doing anything obviously wrong. The woman isn't lying about her mother-in-law. The man isn't disobeying a commandment that says you have to talk to your wife all the time. If you try to preach to them (as they would call it), they'll reject the message and maybe the messenger.

You could take a more psychological approach and try to delve into their past. Maybe the husband is silent because his father didn't show love to him. Maybe the wife complains about her mother-in-law because she lacks self-esteem. If you turned over enough rocks in their past some bugs would crawl out. But there's no certainty you would ever get to the basis of why they behave as they do, or that they would be able to change their behavior if you did. How *is* self-esteem built in a grown woman who lacks it?

Without taking anything away from either the moral or psychological approaches, I would offer another way. It would help a great deal, I believe, if they both learned how to talk. The woman needs to learn to carefully limit her critiques of her mother-in-law. The man needs to learn some ways to say "I love you" so his wife can hear it. Both of them need to learn new ways of bringing up sore subjects without starting fights that make everything worse. If they learned such skills, it might not put an end to all their troubles, but it would be a very big and helpful start. It would stop the bleeding and begin to let their love flow through.

Such training in talking you don't get in school. You get it—if you get it—at home. It is typically transmitted mother to daughter, father to son. Unfortunately, a lot of people miss out. Such training takes time, and it requires confidence on the part of the parents. If they themselves don't know how to talk, they can't very well pass it on.

∞

I am peculiarly and painfully aware of this need for training because I missed out on so much of it. I grew up in a wonderful family, but it was the kind of family where, if you thought someone's opinion was stupid, you said so. We had great debates around the kitchen table, my sisters and brother and parents and I. I learned how to think in my family, but I can't say I learned how to talk. Perhaps this had more to do with my personal makeup than with my family makeup. For whatever reason, I was well into my college years before I learned that when you say to someone that his favorite movie is "incredibly dumb" you may hurt his feelings.

In addition, I was shy. Oftentimes shy people retreat into themselves and give the impression of unfriendly aloofness. I did, and nobody taught me how to compensate for that shyness.

I never had very intimate friendships in high school (can you guess why?), but when I got to college I began to experience closeness in a way I never had. The sheer loneliness of being freshmen far from home drove us together, and I made some wonderful friends.

Sometime in my second or third year I began to understand that others' image of me did not match my image of myself. Others—particularly those who didn't know me well—saw me as stern, aloof, and judgmental. Nobody told me that directly. Once I began to catch on, however, I got the message from all sides.

It pained me deeply, because it wasn't true. I knew what was inside me. I was as aloof as a puppy dog. I was softhearted, if anything. I cared about people. I craved friendship.

At first I felt very hurt that people misjudged me. How could they? As I thought about it, though, I realized that the righteousness of my position didn't matter much. In my writing classes I had learned a thing or two about communication. I knew that if you write a piece that people don't "get," you can't say it is their fault. You have to rewrite it in a different way. You have to find a way to get your point across to your audience.

So I began to try to rewrite my behavior. I began consciously to say nice things to people, to let them know that I appreciated and liked them. I tried to act warmly. I began to hold my tongue when I had something to say that might be construed as critical or snobbish.

I hated it. It felt horribly unnatural. I despised having to watch my words, having to mull over every interaction to see whether I'd handled it well and gotten my message across. Why couldn't I just be myself? I was, I suppose, a true child of the sixties: I believed that simply being sincere was enough. Now I felt that I was acting *insincerely*, putting on an act.

My changes *did* bring noticeably better results, though. People told me I was different. They told me I seemed warmer, happier. People opened up to me. People sought me out. I liked those differences. And I found that I got used to the act I was putting on. Over months and years it grew comfortable. Eventually it became liberating. It became *me*.

For years I have coached youth soccer. Most of the

under-ten kids I get only know how to kick with their right foot. They may be fairly skilled at kicking with their right foot, but when they try to kick left-footed, they look incredibly spastic. Usually they give a pitifully weak kick that dribbles the ball a few yards in front of them. Sometimes they miss the ball entirely and fall on their rears.

As their coach, I know that soccer players have to learn to use both feet. So I encourage them to use the "off" foot, the one that's uncoordinated. There is no magic trick I can teach them. They just have to do it. If they do, they will get better at it, and one day they will feel as natural kicking with the "off" foot as they do with their primary foot. In the end they will become much better soccer players than if they simply continue improving with just one foot.

We ordinarily choose to do the things we're comfortable doing. Sometimes you have to make yourself uncomfortable, do things differently—strange as that may feel—until you become comfortable again. Sometimes you have to kick left-footed. That's what I discovered in college about my ways of relating to people. Spontaneity and sincerity aren't enough. You need to be trained. In fact, it's only the well-trained athlete who can make the spontaneous play. He's the only one who has the skill to see all the options.

∾○∾

We talk about lives being changed from the inside out. My experience is that they are sometimes changed from the outside in. As we change our behavior, it becomes possible for us to feel differently, perceive differently, live differently.

What worries people about such an approach is that it seems calculated and artificial. It seems phony. I am sure that it could be. That wasn't my experience, however. To the contrary, though it *felt* phony, it helped me develop deeper and more authentic relationships with people.

When I learned how to stop putting people off with my seeming aloofness, when I learned how to say that I liked people and to show an interest in their lives, I began to make freer and more open friendships. This in turn made me into a far more confident, friendly person—naturally. I can honestly say that learning how to talk changed my life. It enabled me to be myself.

〜〜

At the same time I was studying and changing the way I talked to people, I was noticing something in my classes. I had a teacher, Jerry Irish, who was a genius at mining dumb comments for gold. I took his seminar in nineteenth-century theology, and I don't think I was the only student at sea among the Schliermachers and Kierkegaards. We made incredibly blundering stabs at answering the thoughtful questions Professor Irish put to us. Often I not only didn't know what my fellow students were trying to say, I wasn't sure they did! But Professor Irish could somehow see a kernel of relevance in those answers, draw it out, and move the whole discussion along. He made us feel that we had remarkable insight—and when he guided our discussion, we did!

There is a considerable art to leading a discussion, I began to see. When I tried to lead Bible studies, I learned that there is also some art to participating.

Every discussion leader knows the troublemakers: the Dominator who won't give anyone else a chance; the Put-Down Artist who corrects others' comments and makes them feel stupid; the Silent One who makes everybody edgy. There are those who love raising impossible questions (free will versus predestination) or who constantly take the discussion far off the subject. There is the Answer Man (or Woman) who shuts everybody up by knowing everything. And so on.

I experienced all these, and learned that a good group discussion depends on skilled participants as well as skilled leaders. Participants do not need to know correct answers, but they do need to know how to carry on a discussion. They must know, in particular, that they need not always talk just because they think they know the answer. They must ask themselves: what good would I do in sharing this Right Answer? How will it affect the people who hear it? Sometimes it's better to keep your mouth shut and let someone else answer. Sometimes it's better to raise another question, to tell a story, to express a feeling.

One of the first things kids learn in school is to put up their hands if they know the answer. First graders are so excited by the chance for their teacher's attention they virtually pull their shoulders out of socket, trying to raise their hands highest. That dynamic continues right through college. Students who think they know the answer speak up, essentially because they hope to impress the teacher. When they ask a question, it is often not because they want to know the answer, but just to show off how acute their minds are. Everybody—teachers and students—competes to establish their place in the pecking order. So the classroom conversations too frequently go nowhere. Teachers and students take turns talking *at* each other. If students knew how to talk, it could be a collaboration, a shared exploration of new knowledge. But how many classes like that can you remember?

It's not just the classroom. It's anywhere people work together by talking things through. When people know how to talk, they not only profit personally. Society profits. What kind of world would it be if every classroom, every business conference, every committee, every school board meeting and every legislative body was dominated by people who knew when and how to speak for the mutual edification of the group? I know this for sure: it would be a world where I wouldn't hate meetings so much.

Take committee meetings. I don't know anyone who enjoys them, and the chief reason is that they take too long to accomplish too little. Sometimes that's for lack of goals and a clear direction. Quite often, however, meetings are overlong because people talk as though they had their hearing aids turned off. There's Rachel, who always has to give her speech about the dangers of going over budget. She's given it ten times, but she doesn't seem to remember. Then Roger, right in the middle of a discussion about publicity, shares his dream of a youth center being built on the old Fresier property. This has nothing to do with the committee's purpose, but it deflects the conversation for fifteen minutes. There's Mattie, who, when asked her opinion, typically says her opinion doesn't matter, which invariably causes Ben, the chairman, to take time to reassure her that her opinion is very important. In the end they're there past 10:00 P.M., and everyone leaves feeling frustrated and tired.

If people knew how to talk, committee meetings would focus on the agenda, comments would build on what's already been said, business would get accomplished, and there would be time afterwards for casual conversation or for prayer.

Take city council meetings. If people knew how to talk, grandstanding would be eliminated. Citizens who came to criticize city government would show, in the tone of their comments, their appreciation and respect for elected officials. Discussion could go back and forth without being stopped cold by someone making a campaign speech. People would actually listen and respond to the points their opponents made, rather than attack their motives. Meetings would be interesting and informative, and more ordinary citizens would participate knowing that their time wouldn't be taken up with pointless arguments. In short, knowing how to talk would help democracy work.

Of course, it's not just knowing. It's wanting to know. There is a moral dimension. Do people really want their conversations to go somewhere? Or would they rather make their speeches, score their points, raise their status?

⤠⚬⤠

By the time I left college, I had realized that the way we talk is vastly important. Looking back, I think this was the critical lesson. I had begun to pay attention. Paying attention is key in learning the way of wisdom.

Two additional elements came years later. One was meeting the woman who became my wife. Popie was (and is) the warmest person I had ever met. I liked her right away, and I wanted her to like me. She obviously did, and she let me know it. But then, she let *everyone* know how much she liked them. She was lavish with her affirmation.

Affirmation is only one way of talking, but it is an extremely important one. Popie's affirmation of others was extravagant. I saw that it made an extraordinary difference in her friends. They were different when she was around them, and they were different *after* she was around them.

I saw this with Karen, a woman with whom Popie shared a house. Karen was quiet, almost reclusive. She was a computer whiz, who loved to stay up all night reading science fiction novels. She was very emotionally intense, but not terribly easy to talk to. Yet Popie was constantly affirming her. If Karen wore interesting clothes, Popie noticed. Popie often pointed out how smart Karen was. "Don't you feel privileged," she would say to a guest, "just to be in the room with someone so *intelligent?*" Most of all, she told Karen how much she liked her. Karen was a person who could easily get overlooked. Popie did not overlook her. She liked her—she made a point of liking her—and she told her so. (She told everyone else, too.) If someone else said something good about Karen, Popie would be sure to pass it on.

Many years later, when Karen was happily married and mother to two delightful children, she called Popie up one day, out of the blue, just to thank her for the gift of those many affirmations. She said they had made a crucial difference in her life. I wasn't surprised. I'd seen the difference. Under Popie's affirmation Karen had gained confidence and warmth. She'd become more relaxed, more herself. She'd become the wonderful person that Popie had always been able to see.

Popie affected lots of people that way. And what was her technique for influencing their lives so powerfully? She said encouraging things to them.

Seeing how Popie affected others (and me), I began to see words as very powerful tools. I had always wanted to be a powerful person. I never knew it was so possible. The key was as close as the words that came out of my mouth.

Anyone—*anyone*—can be a powerful person in the lives of others.

∽o∽

At about the same period of my life, I took a class studying the wisdom literature of the Bible—specifically, the book of Proverbs.

I was slightly familiar with the scriptural proverbs, but I took them about as seriously as I took the American proverbs. Here's an American proverb: "A rolling stone gathers no moss." Here's a biblical proverb: "If a man loudly blesses his neighbor early in the morning, it will be taken as a curse" (27:14). Both are piquant, quaint, and amusing, but I thought of neither as a guide to life or a truth worthy of deep reflection. I liked them but didn't respect them.

When our class looked seriously at the book of Proverbs, however, I was forced to reevaluate my attitude. The sheer number of the biblical proverbs, and the importance they are given in the book's nine-chapter introduction, indicated that this was a source of wisdom that ancient Jews took very seriously.

As I began to study the biblical proverbs, I found all kinds of practical lessons on the very subject I had already begun to study without a textbook. I found that many of the proverbs concern the way we talk. They teach the skill of speaking well in everyday conversation.

That led me to think seriously about another biblical text. "If anyone is never at fault in what he says, he is a perfect man, able to keep his whole body in check," the book of James says.

Perfect? Was that sheer hyperbole? I had always thought so, but now I looked again. James underlines the thought with two comparisons. "When we put bits into the mouths of horses to make them obey us, we can turn the whole animal. Or take ships as an example. Although they are so large and are driven by strong winds, they are steered by a very small rudder wherever the pilot wants to go. Likewise the tongue is a small part of the body . . ." (3:3–5). James goes on to warn about the evil that a tongue can do, but these first metaphors are clearly positive in thrust.

They suggest that we can control our lives by controlling our tongues. They suggest—this is truly startling—that if we were able to consistently choose our words well, we could make our lives all that we want them to be, and all that God means them to be.

Do you feel that your life is out of control? Are forces around you and inside you too strong? Is it all too complex? James suggests, through these metaphors, that sheer will and strength of character will never enable you to get your life going in the right direction. You cannot direct either a horse or a ship by pushing. They are too big and unwieldy. You must use—skillfully—small instruments of control. For horses, the bit. For ships, the rudder. For human beings, the tongue.

In this book, we will explore some fundamental strategies for turning your life in a new direction through the skillful use of your tongue.

CHAPTER TWO

Taking Inventory

For your words you will be acquitted, and by your words you will be condemned.

(Matthew 12:37)

My sons, Chase and Silas, do not always get along. (Surprised?) Here's the scene: Chase, who is three years older than Silas, sneers at his brother's knowledge of baseball. Silas, in tears of frustration, throws his baseball glove on the ground. And now I am in Chase's face. "It's not what you said, it's how you said it, Chase. Do you have any idea how you sounded? Do you understand the way you affect your brother when you talk like that? I wish you could hear yourself talk."

But then I think: he's not the only one. *I* do a lot of talking without thinking. How often do *I* pop someone's bubble with careless words? How well do *I* hear my own tone of voice?

Take Your Inventory

Most of us don't know how we talk. We just open our mouths, and out it comes. We talk all the time, all day, in every situation. Monday morning in the office we talk about who won the football game. Bumping into a friend in the hallway, we discuss who's in charge of the carpool. At lunch we fall into a discussion about a new cop show on TV. Seeing a daughter hunched over her math homework when we arrive home, we tell her about the terrible algebra teacher we had. Listening to the late-night news, we pour out to a spouse the reasons why we don't trust the government.

If you typed up everything an ordinary person said during

the day, it could easily add up to a book's worth of material. Considering how much talking we do, it's amazing how little attention we pay. That book you spoke today—how much of it would you want to read?

Only certain kinds of talking get our attention. People *do* sometimes study how to make a speech. You can take classes in that—Speech 101. And some careers require paying attention to communication skills. Counselors and psychologists learn techniques for getting people to open up. Ministers worry about style as well as content when they prepare their sermons. Teachers consider how to communicate their subject matter.

Nobody studies, however, the speech that makes up ninety percent of our days: the ordinary words between parents and children, husbands and wives, between friends, between neighbors, between coworkers. There are no classes on conversational skills.

We may learn, as children, that it's wrong to "talk dirty," or to use certain ugly words. We may learn that it's wrong to tell a lie. We may learn not to gossip or to reveal secrets. On the positive side, we may learn that it's important to express ourselves, to let people know how we're feeling.

That's it. It's a terribly thin education. Especially if it's true that by skillfully controlling our words we can take control of our lives and move in new directions.

∽∽o∽∽

Think back over the last twenty-four hours. How many of your words can you remember? If you're like most people, you remember very few.

Most people remember the words they used in a quarrel. They can recall the heart-chilling rebuke they gave someone who deserved it. They also remember unusually warm and loving words—if, say, they cuddled up to their spouse and gave a winning compliment.

However, since most people don't fight every day, and since most people rarely go out of their way to stroke others verbally, most people can't remember a thing they said all day. It's a blank. They remember talking to people, they remember the general drift of what was discussed, but they have no idea of the specific words they used, or whether they used them well or badly.

In fact, most people can't tell you what words they used ten minutes after a conversation.

Your first task is to turn this around. You can't change the way you talk—and thus your life—if you don't pay attention. You have to learn to listen—listen to *yourself*. You have to take inventory of your words, find out what's good, what's bad, and what's pointless. Only then can you make your words serve your purposes in life.

For example, in relating to my thirteen-year-old daughter, Katie, I know what I want. I want very much to communicate my love and establish a climate of warmth and encouragement, even while I am sometimes setting limits, correcting her behavior, and challenging her to make mature decisions for herself.

To some degree, every conversation between us—even the "Hi, how did you sleep?" of the morning—contributes to my success in these goals. If I set a grumpy, uncommunicative tone first thing in the morning, it may flavor the whole day. On the other hand, if I make our first meeting of the morning a small but distinct pleasure, I may build a foundation for more significant communication. So I need to evaluate *all* my conversation with her—both the heavy and the light, the trivial and the significant. I even need to evaluate the silences.

Sometimes when I'm driving her to a school function, there's a lot of quiet between us. Frankly, I sometimes welcome that, because conversation comes hard at times. When I try to get a conversation going by asking questions, I may only irritate Katie. I need to ask myself: Is this a fruitful silence? I need to give her space, but I also need to be in touch with her, and she with me. I need to evaluate: Where is that balance between giving space and making contact? How can I start a conversation without seeming to pry into her life?

When I really think about it, it is very complicated knowing how to talk with my thirteen-year-old daughter. But then, I could say the same thing of nearly any other person in my life.

Some Basic Techniques

To take inventory of your words, some aids may help. One of the best is a notebook. I like to use a very small, wallet-sized spiral notebook. It fits in a pocket, and you can write in it even while standing in a crowded elevator. (That's why newspaper reporters often use them.)

You can't take notes on everything you say in a day. That's just too much stuff to write down. You can, however, focus on one or two people and try to jot down notes on every interaction you have with them. Take, for example, a child, a spouse, or a coworker—anyone you're trying to relate with better. Make as complete an accounting as possible. Over the course of two or three days try to build a fairly complete record of how you talk with that person. Write down the gist of your conversations. As much as possible, write down the actual words. It might help to note the following information to jog your memory later:

Date:
Person I talked with:
Place:
Purpose of conversation:
How I felt about the conversation:
What we said:

Don't worry, by the way, about whether you're self-consciously changing the way you talk during this "trial period." You probably are, but that's okay. Your old habits will find their way into your conversation, even when you try to avoid them. Habits of speech are much too strong to repress for long.

Another slightly different approach: take time at the end of each day to jot down everything you can remember about the conversations of the day. After doing this for a few days, you'll find that you remember more. You'll tune in more while the conversations are going on, so they'll stick in your mind. In a week, you'll have written down a lot of words.

A third approach is to use a tape recorder. You can, for example, turn it on during a meal and record the whole conversation. A tape recorder will probably feel intrusive at first, but after a while you'll find that you can ignore the machine and carry on a fairly normal conversation. The advantage of a tape recorder is, of course, that it catches everything; it doesn't have a selective memory. When you listen to the recording, you'll hear some comments you may not remember at all—and probably some you won't be very pleased by. The disadvantage of the tape recorder—besides the intrusiveness—is that you may focus too much on the sound of your voice. (Few of us sound like radio announcers.) Another disadvantage is that a tape recorder won't catch other "on-the-fly" remarks that need attention: the greetings, the good-byes, the comments as you go out the door.

Actually, you can use all three of these approaches at once if you like. You simply want a fairly accurate, fairly complete record of *all* the things you say. Then you can analyze it. Without such a record you end up evaluating how you *feel* about your conversational skills, rather than the actual words you use. Feelings go up and down. The actual quality of the words, good or bad, tends to be fairly consistent.

It's that way with any art. A painter's emotions about his work may soar one day, dip another. You won't necessarily be able to tell by looking at his paintings, however. The quality of the work stays approximately the same from day to day. If you want to evaluate a painter, don't ask him how he feels about his work. Look at his paintings.

Listen to Yourself

Listening to yourself can be quite a shock! Many people are appalled when they first tune in to their own conversation. They're appalled by the harsh words they use without thinking. They're sickened by the gossip, the insincerity. Even more, they're aghast at how banal their conversations are. With all the messages we need to give each other—messages of love, compassion, warning—most people manage to spend their words on things they don't care about at all. They chitchat a lot.

Confronting your own words is not comfortable. Unfortunately, there are plenty of ways to discount the grim realities. Here are a few:

"*I didn't mean it.*" You may find that you made some severe comments to your spouse. "You're just like your father," you said. Or, "Every time I turn around you've got a list of things you want me to do. I'm sick of it!"

"I didn't mean that," you say now. "I was just blowing off steam. I was just mad. I'd had a bad morning."

The trouble is, you *did* mean it. Jesus said, "The good man brings good things out of the good stored up in his heart, and the evil man brings evil things out of the evil stored up in his heart. For out of the overflow of his heart his mouth speaks" (Luke 6:45). To face your own harsh words is to confront the overflow of anger and self-righteousness in yourself. So long as you discount these words, you can't get to the root of them—and the anger will almost certainly continue to overflow until you do.

"*That was just talk.*" People try to shoo away their words like flies at the dinner table. "Words don't amount to anything," they suggest. "Watch what I do, not what I say."

If that's true, why is it that couples getting a divorce so often remember what their partner *said?* Why do so many people come into my wife's counseling office remembering with horrifying clarity a comment a parent made twenty years ago?

Words *do* matter. It is with words, principally, that we build or destroy relationships. Often it's the throwaway words—the casual passing remarks—that bury themselves deep into another person's heart.

"*I was only joking.*" I grew up using a lot of sarcasm. Then a post-college housemate confronted me with the message behind my humor. He said that humor often contained a put-down, that it often downgraded people or kept them at a distance. I fiercely denied it. I was sure he was just being sensitive.

He got me to listen to myself, though. I saw that he was right. I liked to tease him about always being late. I thought it was amusing. He didn't. Underneath the humor was a statement: I am well organized, you are incompetent. He heard the message.

If you listen closely, you'll often find a message inside humor—a message that isn't really nice. In fact, humorous put-downs are doubly potent, because a person who takes offense "has no sense of humor," or "can't take a joke." So he or she loses twice.

Skillfully used, humor can be wonderfully helpful. Sometimes it enables people to talk about a subject they couldn't otherwise face. Sometimes it defuses tension. But humor is never "just a joke." For good or evil, it has a meaning that you have to consider when you take inventory of your words. If people are stung by your words, it's not "just a joke." It's serious.

"They know what I meant." People often claim that their friends or family members possess a special ability to decode their words, so that they get a different message than the words literally convey.

For example, when you say, "You jerk!" your friend is supposed to know that you mean, "You're my buddy and I love to clown around with you."

Or, "If you say that one more time, I'm getting a divorce," should be interpreted to mean, "I'm having a hard time dealing with the way you say that, but of course I'm deeply committed to you."

Or, "Do you want to go out to dinner?" should be correctly

interpreted to mean, "There's nobody I'd rather spend time with than you. I love you. You're the greatest."

Or, "There's no way you're going out of this house in that dress," should be understood by your daughter to mean, "You're a very attractive girl, and I worry that guys are going to get the wrong message when they see you in that dress."

To all of these examples, I can only respond, "Perhaps they get the message you think they should. But perhaps not. Perhaps they only *sometimes* understand. And wouldn't it be better if your family and friends didn't need a code book to interpret your words? Wouldn't it make more sense to say what you actually mean?"

"Every word I said was true." People use this defense when their hard words have started a fight. They're often correct; the hard words were literally true. The trouble is, meaningful relationships require more than "the truth, the whole truth, and nothing but the truth." A living room isn't a courtroom.

Some truths don't need to be said at all. Others need to be said in just the right way. And what about the truths you leave out? People often tell the grim truth (as they see it) but don't include the happier truths that fill out the picture. Like with my children. I can be terrifyingly truthful when listing their failings. But do I say the larger truth that they are delightful, responsible persons? When I am being terribly truthful about their failings, don't I sometimes give an inaccurate impression about who they are and what they mean to me?

Analyze Your Inventory

Many people resist taking a word inventory. They fear that if they started counting their words, they'll repress their personalities. They'd become guarded, programmed, rule-bound. When I suggest taking inventory on your words, it sounds a lot like accounting, and we all know what free spirits accountants are!

Taking inventory is just the beginning, however. What comes next isn't rule-bound, it's artistic. Speech is an art form by which you build relationships, express your personality, create a life to admire. When you don't pay attention, careless words may do just the opposite: destroy relationships, express your worst side, let your life slump into chaos.

There is no one "right" way to talk, any more than there is a "right" way to paint a picture. Different personalities will find their own style. A giddy personality won't become sober and thoughtful. Neither will a quiet, deep person begin showering others with extravagant compliments. Each one must find his or her own way. You work with the raw material of your own makeup.

But "work" is the key word. Words are tools that we work with. As with all tools, there are right and wrong ways to use them. You don't use a screwdriver as a chisel. You always measure before you use a saw. These are invariable rules we all must follow. The end results, however, may be very different. One person may create a sailboat, another a swing set. The skill of both in using their tools will always show nonetheless.

When you've taken your inventory, therefore, take time to reflect. Write down answers to these questions: What are your goals with each person you're relating to regularly? In each environment—home, work, neighborhood, school— what are you trying to build? Then look over the words you've inventoried. Which ones contributed most to your achieving these goals? Which ones hurt? Your paper might look like this:

The person (or environment) I care about:
The message(s) I want to send:
Words I used that contributed to my message:
Words I used that contradicted my message:
Words I *didn't* say but would like to:

After you've analyzed your inventory, you may feel distressed and confused. Like a kid who has struck out three times in a row, you'll know you're not doing well, but you might not be sure how to fix the problem. Take courage. There are specific steps you can take to move ahead. While the art of speech can't be fully taught—after all, it is an *art*—the basics can be.

CHAPTER THREE

Toxic Talk:
Harsh Words and Lies

Reckless words pierce like a sword,
but the tongue of the wise brings healing.
(Proverbs 12:18)

Suppose a grocer takes inventory of his store. Buried in the bottom of his meat section he finds five packages of overripe hamburger. They have somehow sat there for two weeks, turning green.

What should the grocer do with this rotting meat? No one would argue the answer. He should get rid of it immediately! Furthermore, he should make certain that he never again neglects his meat section. He may have a beautiful store stocked with gorgeous produce, but rotten meat will spoil his business. Any customer who spots that greening goop will want to walk out of the store and never return.

It's the same with talk. Less than one percent of a person's word inventory can ruin the effect of all the rest. I've known people whose words could charm a snake out of its hole, people who are gracious in ninety-nine percent of what they say. But there is a toxic streak in their words that spoils the rest.

If you talk to such people, you'll usually find they don't realize the impact of those toxic words. In fact, they're sometimes proud of their toughness, their candid truth-telling.

The problem is not restricted to a few mean-mouthed people. Almost everybody contributes some toxic talk, at least occasionally. And almost everybody has been poisoned by hearing it. As I've mentioned before, almost everybody can recall words that stung, words that crushed the spirit, words that left them feeling hopeless and desolate for days.

How many people remember being told as children that they were stupid? How many people remember being told as adults that they were overweight? That it is their fault that their children have problems?

It's amazing how often people remember having such words said to them, and yet how seldom people remember *saying* such words to others. We usually don't mean to hurt people. The words just pop out without our planning. We forget them. But those who hear them don't.

Sometimes words have to hurt. When you confront real problems, you must face painful realities. That's far different, however, from toxic talk. Toxic talk doesn't lead to dialogue—it stops it. Toxic talk is usually spoken in haste or in anger. The poison lingers on long after the emotions are gone.

Your first task is to identify the toxic words in your speech and get rid of them.

Harsh Words

> A gentle answer turns away wrath,
> but a harsh word stirs up anger.
>
> *(Proverbs 15:1)*

Name-calling

Some words can simply be eliminated from your vocabulary because they amount to name calling. Calling someone a whore, a racist, or a Nazi, for example—those are fighting words. Any racially-loaded term—such as nigger, boy, gook, wog, kike, the list goes on—makes a bad situation impossible.

Some words are subtler but still hurtful. I believe the

word "stupid" need never be used in a personal way. (Dumb, idiot, and fool can be dropped too.) The government may be stupid, but your brother-in-law is not. I don't like to hear the president being called an idiot, regardless of whether he's a Republican or a Democrat. The habit of name-calling is catching. It's corrosive. Children who hear such put-downs will learn to use them.

Sometimes name-calling can be very subtle. Take the word "insensitive." Nine times out of ten it's a put-down. If you tell someone he's "insensitive," what can he do about it? How can he disprove it? By crying? (The same might be said of the opposite word, "sensitive." It's often used disparagingly, as in "He's *so* sensitive.")

Unfortunately, we can't post an all-time list of words that should never be used. The creativity of name-calling is inexhaustible. There's forever a new way to put someone down. It's not that hard to detect name-calling if your ears are tuned to it, though. Name-calling focuses on the character of the individual rather than on the particular problem at hand. It claims, "You're a liar," rather than saying, "You lied to me about where you were last night." To detect name-calling, ask yourself: Is there anything really constructive about this word? Does it help us understand our problem? Or does it simply raise everybody's anger a notch?

Words that wear on the soul

Some words don't make anybody mad; they're just ugly and negative. Used frequently, they leave people tired and discouraged. "Shut up," for example, is an abrupt and angry way to ask for quiet. In our house it's not allowed. For the same reason, we don't use swear words or vulgar words. (I could list them, but my publisher wouldn't like it.) They don't help, and who needs them? The English language has plenty of expletives and adjectives that aren't coarse.

Words that take the heart out of people

One I've already talked about is "divorce," used by a married couple when fighting. You may use it to get your partner's attention, but it usually gets more than attention. It's like pulling out a gun in the middle of an argument: suddenly the focus isn't on the issue you were arguing over but on the gun. Saying "divorce" can instantly transform a marital quarrel into a death struggle. It reveals (or seems to, anyway) a lack of commitment to the marriage and a fundamental lack of love. It can take the heart out of your partner. I believe marriage partners would be better off never using the word with each other. They may happen to think about it, but they should not say it.

Another word to take the heart out of a person is "disappoint." A friend called me up after being out of touch for a couple of years. We'd lost contact after I'd disagreed with some ethical choices he'd made. Now he wanted to reestablish our friendship, but first he wanted to talk honestly about our disagreement.

As we talked, the problem came down to one word. When we'd disagreed, I'd said I was disappointed with him. To me it had merely expressed the pain I had felt in seeing a close friend fail. I had felt really saddened by his choices. I had been, well, disappointed. To him, however, that word had conveyed more than sadness; it had conveyed fundamental, damning disapproval. "Disappoint" had hit him in the gut, and he had not been able to catch his breath again.

I can't explain rationally why that word had triggered so much. But I can imagine, intuitively, how it would have. It's a word that communicates boundless and unchangeable failure: "You are less than I thought." "I can't respect you anymore." I hadn't wanted to convey that. But that word had. I'm not sure my friendship will ever fully recover from "disappoint." I know I will not use it ever again with a friend. I hope I will never use it with my children.

Words that overstate the point

When you're upset, it's easy to exaggerate. Sometimes we think we have to overstate things to get our point across. Actually, exaggeration usually keeps us from getting our point across. It stops communication, because the person is so upset by the exaggeration, they can't focus on the real point.

For example, my wife and I have different philosophies of time. She hates to be early. I hate to be late. Her idea of the right time to arrive at a movie is as the credits roll. She likes to get to church as people stand for the opening hymn, to reach the jetway as the last boarding call is made.

Okay, okay, so I'm already exaggerating. But not much.

When we talk about our different views of time, it does not help if I say, "Not once in our married life have we been on time for a meeting." It does not help if she says, "Every single time we go anywhere together, you start off the evening uptight." Such statements are so exaggerated that we both find it easy to avoid the issue and fight over the exaggeration.

It's important, when you're dealing with problems, to be as precise and down-to-earth as possible. It helps to avoid certain words and phrases that go with exaggeration:

Always and *never,* as in "You never balance your checkbook" or "You are always late." Hardly anybody *always* or *never* does anything. And such exaggerations leave no room for hope. If I'm late ninety percent of the time, at least I get it right ten percent of the time. Maybe I could expand on that good behavior. If I'm *always* late, it looks like I'm hopeless.

Just like your father/mother. These exaggerations are particularly common in marital battles, if my experience is any guide. Nobody is *just* like his father or mother, and saying so is almost bound to get a person's hackles up. In one phrase you've pigeonholed them and insulted one of their parents.

Words that rub salt into a wound

There's such a thing as old business. If you bring up old mistakes, old fights, old differences, old flames, you could be distracting from what's at hand here and now. More importantly, you could be rubbing salt into an old wound.

Each person has his or her own unique sensitivities. You have to know him or her well to know what wounds are raw. It might be her college grades, it might be sexual abuses he suffered from as a child. When you know what's sensitive, though, you delete the words that will rub salt into the wound.

I made a friend in college whom I lovingly referred to as "fat old Frank." Frank wasn't fat, just slightly on the ample side. I must have called him "fat old Frank" with all good intentions for six months before I discovered he was deeply sensitive about his weight. I was mortified! Every single time I had opened my mouth with that greeting I had offended him! It must have happened twenty times!

Other people are sensitive about their intelligence. Maybe they got teased as children. So when you make a joke about a word they misspelled, or about balancing the checkbook, it *hurts*. Obviously, you can't be aware of every person's unique sensitivities. But for those you love, those you live with, and those you work with closely, it's important to know the words that cause them pain.

Words (and tone) that communicate personal disgust

There's a way of talking that consigns another person to worthlessness. It gives them the feeling that they are useless to you. You may feel it. Don't say it. Your feelings may change. The words will linger forever.

For example, I guess every married person on the face of the earth has had a moment or two when they don't find their partner desirable. She's overweight and looks like a slob. His face looks like a horse's. (Why didn't I notice on the wedding day?)

Keep these thoughts to yourself and ask God to help your feelings to change.

❧o❧

Getting rid of harsh words requires that you control your mouth. You may have to talk less. An Old Testament proverb says, "When words are many, sin is not absent" (Proverbs 10:19). Strong, silent types aren't better people, but they *do* get in trouble less often. Another proverb says (I'm paraphrasing), "Even a fool seems wise if he keeps his mouth shut" (Proverbs 17:28).

You may also have to slow down. Talk only as fast as your brain can keep up. Take a split second to think before you begin to speak. If you're not sure whether your words will hurt someone's feelings, play it safe and don't say them. You'll get another chance to say what you really mean to say; but once toxic words are out of your mouth, you can't get them back.

When you're talking with someone, make sure you hear them all the way out before you answer. A lot of painful, wounding words come when you don't fully understand what's being said—you jump to conclusions. Great effort is required to *listen* when you've got something you're burning to say.

These changes may suggest that you must bottle up your feelings, keep them inside, never express them. That is just what you must *not* do. Strong friendships can only be built between people able to express strong emotions. Inevitably, if you are close, that involves anger. As my father used to remind me, "If you dance close, you will sometimes step on toes."

You don't eliminate harsh words in order to keep angry feelings inside. You eliminate harsh words in order to keep the channels open for strong emotions. Harsh words close channels. They are too painful; people shut down. They won't hear you anymore, because your words have hurt them. They won't risk exposing their wounds to you again.

Anger must be expressed, but in a positive and constructive way. It is still anger, and painful to hear. But when expressed well, anger will draw two people closer. We will come back to this in Chapter 6: Talking about Trouble.

⌘

I haven't mentioned one last reason why some people use harsh words: they like to quarrel. They actually prefer to fight it out rather than to negotiate.

At first that seems perverse. Who likes fighting? Why not prefer peace and quiet? There is a logic to fighting, though. It's less work. You say what you feel like saying. Instead of painting a picture, you throw a bucket of paint on the canvas. You express your feelings and walk away, leaving somebody else to clean up the mess.

If you choose fighting persistently (and that's what someone who fights all the time is doing—choosing it), you're using a strategy that avoids relationships. It's a sign that you're afraid of people—perhaps afraid of the pain and effort real relationships require. Fights enable you to keep people at a distance. Some people's conversational style is the equivalent of the kid who walks across the school playground with fists doubled up, looking for a fight.

If this is you, you have to go deeper than confronting your conversational style. You have to face your personality style. You may need some thorough, professional counseling to help you do it.

Lies

The Lord detests lying lips,
but he delights in men who are truthful.
(Proverbs 12:22)

Lies are a second form of toxic talk. Like harsh words, they must be eliminated.

I guess almost everybody agrees that lying is wrong. It's against the Ten Commandments, for heaven's sake. Yet lying is awfully common, especially if you count the "little white lies." For example:

"Where were you last night?"

"I was just driving around." *Not to mention stopping by Mary's house.*

Or "I couldn't get it done because I was feeling sick." *Sick of working on it, that is.*

The first question that arises is: Are these actually lies? You did, after all, drive around last night. You actually did feel a bit sick. These statements are not untrue, even if someone draws an incorrect conclusion from them.

I have heard some ornate discussions about whether something was actually a lie or not. That's all a waste of time. One famous definition puts all such discussions out the door: "A lie is an attempt to deceive." You may not have said a factually untrue word, but if you were trying to lead someone astray, making them (or letting them) think something other than the truth, you were lying. That's why courts require witnesses to tell not merely the truth but the *whole* truth.

A second question: Are these lies really a big deal? Surely some deceptions are harmless, even helpful. If a woman asks me whether I like her new hairdo, do I have to say I hate it? Is it a great sin to say it's terrific?

The answer to the first question is no; you do not have to tell someone you hate her hair. But I would insist that the answer to the second question is yes. Yes, it is a sin to say what you know is not true. Even the smallest lie counts as a lie. Maybe the question of whether you like someone's hair or who took the last piece of pie isn't of epic importance. Maybe the reason you didn't come straight home from work really isn't anybody's business but your own. Nevertheless, a lie remains a lie, and as such is very serious indeed.

That's because our words are very serious indeed. They are the chief building blocks of relationships. They make the world we live in. If we lie, we create an untrustworthy world. In a world full of lies you can't trust anybody, and you never know where you stand. *All* lies contribute to mistrust.

Even the woman with the new hairdo. If you lie to her, she will eventually learn that when you say you love her hair, you really don't mean it. She may prefer this fiction to the truth. But when compliments become meaningless, and everybody says they love your hair whether they do or not, then conversation begins to lose its meaning.

Lies are like counterfeit money. The authorities won't say, "You were only making a few twenty dollar bills, which is such a minute fraction of the national economy as to be insignificant. No big deal." Counterfeiting is always serious, because if people lost trust in the money supply, it would drastically affect all business relationships. Similarly, when people doubt the reliability and trustworthiness of others' words, distrust begins to pervade their relationships.

How do you answer the woman who asks whether you like her hair? I certainly wouldn't say I hate it—even if the woman were my wife and I really did hate it. My first reply would be to try to respond to the true meaning of her question. Most of the time a woman who asks such a question is seeking reassurance. You can answer that by saying, "It's quite a change, and it will probably take me a while to get used to it. But you know what? I like you in any hairdo."

If she persists—if she just has to know what I think about her hair—I'll say something like this, with a smile: "It's not my favorite."

⚬⚭⚬

If you grew up in a strict home like mine, lies are out of the question. Telling the truth was a deadly serious requirement under all circumstances. It was far better to be caught, say, stealing than to be caught lying about it. Consequently, I just don't lie. Lying doesn't even occur to me—or, I am pretty sure, to any of my siblings.

Which makes it all the more remarkable to me how prevalent lying is. People lie at the drop of a hat. They lie even when they have no reason for lying. Mostly these are "little white lies." And—I freely admit it—many of the lies are done to avoid a quarrel. The truth—that the boss is in but doesn't want to take your call—would upset you, so her secretary says she's not in. It would hurt your mother's feelings if she knew the real reason you weren't coming for Thanksgiving—you despise those drawn-out family meals, especially when she cooks—so you tell her you have an important presentation coming up and you just can't spare the time. These are well-meaning lies. They intend good, not harm.

But this morass is endless. One lie leads to another. Your mother finds out that you went elsewhere for Thanksgiving, and so you have to make up even more elaborate fictions. Sometime, somewhere, somebody realizes that you're not completely truthful. From that point on, how can they tell when you're truthful and when you're not? Distrust seeps in.

Lies keep people at a distance. They insist: I will manage my life, and nobody else will even know enough about what I do to question it. Lying is a philosophy of complete individualism. Lying keeps other people out of your life.

This doesn't mean that you must be bluntly truthful all the time. First, you can tell the truth tactfully. You need not say that the boss gave explicit instructions that she didn't want to talk to Mr. Smith; you can simply say she's not available and ask if you can help in some way. When your mother asks why you are not coming for Thanksgiving, you are not required to say that you can't stand holidays at her house. You can say, "At this point in our family's life we feel it's better for us to spend that time alone," or "I'd rather spend time with you, Mom, on a day when there's not so much going on." That may lead to other, more difficult questions—but those questions can begin some really helpful communication.

There's a skill to this, of course: the skill of using words well. Some people are naturally good at it. Everybody can improve with practice.

Second, there's the skill (and confidence) involved in simply not answering a question.

I learned this from toddlers. If you ask a toddler a question he doesn't want to answer, he will simply appear to have grown temporarily deaf.

Mother: "Willy, what did you do at Grandma's house?"

Willy: "Can I have a cookie?"

Or, "I love you, Mom!"

Or, "I saw a rainbow!"

It is simply amazing how often kids get away with this. The question is forgotten, the conversation proceeds.

I have tried the same strategy with adults and found that it works with stunning effectiveness. You simply remain silent or go on with the conversation as though nothing had been said. Nine times out of ten that will be the end of the question.

Even if someone follows up point-blank, "Why won't you answer my question?" you don't *have* to answer. Nobody can make you answer a question you don't want to answer. They can't pry your mouth open and force you to respond.

Some questions deserve to be ignored. For example, teenagers get asked in school whether they are virgins. Embarrassed by the question, they are tempted to lie. I teach them that the correct answer is "None of your business." Or "That's private." Or "I don't discuss that." This is a more direct approach than simply ignoring the question. I recommend the more direct response because I think teenagers need to be assertive about their sexual values. The value here is: sexual experiences should not be discussed like the weekend's football scores. It's worthwhile to make that case. There are other situations where such an assertion is helpful. With a perpetually nosy father, for example, you may need to politely insist, "Dad, Carol and I consider it a private matter when we are going to have kids. (Or how much money we made last year. Or what we were fighting about.) I'd rather you didn't ask me any more." On the other hand, you don't have to create fuss over every question you don't want to answer. That's when ignoring the question, keeping silent, or simply changing the subject is a better way.

In the short run, lies are easier. Just as, in the short run, it's easier for chemical companies to dump their wastes in the river. But toxics, even in trace amounts, are destructive. You are best off to eliminate them at their source.

∾o∾

Toxic words—harsh words and lies—are so common a form of pollution that most people shrug them off. But they do real, deep damage. You cannot eliminate them from your world, but you can eliminate them from your mouth. It is not foreordained that your friends get their feelings hurt by your mouth. You do not have to burden your children's memory with harsh words that stick to them twenty years from now. Your marriage need not be perpetually troubled by the angry words that pop out of your mouth. You can be a person whose speech is gentle, hardly ever hurtful.

Lies are not inevitable either. You can be known as a person of (tactful) truth. You can stand out as a person who your friends know will say (thoughtfully) what you really believe. You can rise above a generation that treats truth casually.

In short, you can become a different person.

CHAPTER FOUR

The Power of Praise

An anxious heart weighs a man down,
but a kind word cheers him up.

(Proverbs 12:25)

Twenty-five years ago Merlin Carothers published a small book called *The Power of Praise*. His message was simple but profound. Carothers maintained that Christians should praise God in every circumstance, however bad. He told story after story about people whose lives were in a mess until they began simply to praise God. Their lives changed miraculously.

Carothers made a huge impact, even though he went overboard a bit. He implied that people should praise God *for* the problems in their lives, a practice that would have us ultimately praising God for evil he wants very much to eradicate. God does not desire our praise for sexual abuse, for murder, for cancer.

But God certainly wants us praising him in the midst of such evils. And Carothers was absolutely correct that praise—simple praise—revolutionizes our lives. When we praise God, we're doing exactly what we were created to do. It's like putting a locomotive on its track. When we praise God, we stop spinning our wheels, and start moving in the right direction.

The old catechism put it superbly: "The chief end of man is to glorify God and enjoy him forever." We are made to give glory to God and to enjoy him. We do that in many ways, but especially through our words—when we praise him.

∽◦∾

Praise also helps our relationship with our children. In this psychological age we've learned this lesson well: children need affirmation.

When one of my kids comes home from kindergarten with a great, sprawling dinosaur painted on brown art paper, I tell her how it delights me. (I don't point out that it is indistinguishable from the bear she painted last week.) I tell my children I love them. I admire their abilities in every way possible. It doesn't matter that there are other children smarter and quicker and more beautiful. I praise my children for the good that God has put in them, without comparing them to anyone else. It's very important for them to believe in themselves and to know that they are loved. Praise increases their confidence and draws us closer together.

You most clearly see that by looking at children who grow up *without* affirmation. Some children don't remember their parents saying "I love you." They remember chiefly words of criticism. Such children often grow up plagued by guilt and self-doubt. Even as adults many can hardly grasp that they are beautiful and capable and marvelous. Many have a hard time getting it through their skulls that they are God-made.

⋙⋘

It's very interesting: we recognize the importance of praise in relating to children. We see its importance in relating to God. But people often don't grasp its significance in relating to anyone else—their marriage partners, their brothers and sisters, their friends, their coworkers, their parents. Yet words of praise are, I am convinced, the most powerful words that we have at our disposal. In all our relationships, praise makes an astonishing difference.

I know what a difference praise makes because I have felt its impact in my own life. I learned about praise from Popie, my wife, long before we were married.

We were just friends then; I was merely one of a great crowd of admirers. Popie was quite a personality. She had an accent from the deep South and an extravagant way of talking. Everybody loved her, including me. She referred to things by their initials and used archaic English. "My S-in-L is laden with child," she would say, meaning that her sister-in-law was pregnant. Popie had style.

Not just anybody could bring off her style of conversation. She was quite a show, buoyant and cheerful and lavishly positive. Popie was quintessentially herself and happy about it.

I noticed a thread that ran through all her relations with people. She told people what she liked about them. She admired them publicly. She did it to me. It felt absolutely marvelous to have this wonderful, extraordinary girl saying admiring things about me. I didn't know quite how to take it, but I knew that I liked it. Being around Popie was like basking in sunshine. I felt freer, I acted freer. I was funnier, wiser, friendlier, kinder, and more generous when I was under her influence.

She praised many people, not just me. It was hard to figure this out at first: if she said such warm and positive things to so many others, was she sincere? Did she mean it with me? I came to see, however, that love and admiration were not limited for her. Popie saw a lot to like in people, and what she enjoyed in one did not take anything away from another. To her, people were not in competition. It was not necessary to conserve her words of praise. Many people could be beautiful, funny, wise and likable, all at once. She didn't praise people to mark out her special favorites. She praised people because she liked to and because she believed it was the thing to do.

What most startled me was the realization that Popie was a powerful person. She was powerful mainly because she was brave enough and selfless enough to praise other people. She didn't weigh whether they reciprocated. She didn't worry about seeming foolish. Without a trace of self-consciousness she told them—and me—what she liked about them and how much she liked them. It changed them. People not only warmed up when around her, but they were different after they had been around her. She left a residue in their lives. They were better. *I* was better.

I had wanted to make a difference in the world. I had thought in terms of holding influential positions, writing great and wise literature, strategizing important programs. Popie's way stunned me. I saw that anybody could do what she did. So how come nobody did?

⨾⨾⨾

For many people—and certainly for me—praising others doesn't come naturally. I felt like an idiot when I first began imitating Popie and telling my friends that I liked them, that they meant a lot to me. I felt even more foolish when I grew specific and spelled out *how* they mattered to me. The deeper and more significant the affirmation, the more red-faced and stuttery I became.

My friends definitely liked it, however. I was encouraged and kept at it. Praise gradually became more natural. Of course, I had to find my own way of doing it. I definitely couldn't bring off Popie's style.

Eventually I developed my own approach, one that felt comfortable. I look back and wonder how I ever managed without it. How mean, how lacking in grace all my relationships would be without the simple, natural ability to tell people how I like them! I'm not claiming to be great at it. I'll never be as good as my wife. Nonetheless, affirmation and praise became a fundamental pillar of my conversational skills. When my children and I are struggling to get along, when a friend is low, when Popie and I are out of synchrony, I look for something to affirm—something specific and meaningful.

～○～

Praise matters everywhere, not just in marriage; but marriages seem to be the saddest cases when praise is lacking.

Often marriage partners can remember back to their courting days, when it was all different. Back then they communicated admiration and appreciation effortlessly. Just the way they looked at each other told the story! But once married they let it lapse. The few compliments they share now are weak and habitual; there's no charge in them. Mostly they nag or grump or just carry on day-to-day, businesslike conversations.

It's sad, because when you don't get affirmation from your spouse, where can you get it? Men love to hear that their wives admire them: their muscles, their brains, their parenting, their looks. Women love to hear that their husbands adore them: their beauty, their love for children, their business skills, their organization. Praise never gets old. You can hear it again and again even while your hair turns gray and your energy fades. Praise sustains a marriage through the rough patches and puts a glow on the best moments.

All too often, though, partners don't affirm each other. Why not?

Because they were seldom affirmed themselves and never learned the habit.

Because they're embarrassed.

Because they're afraid they'll make their partner conceited.

Because they think their partner already knows how they feel and doesn't need to hear it.

Because they have mixed feelings, and it's hard to say nice things when you feel so much anger.

Because they don't know what to say.

Because they're great at *doing* for others and have never seen the necessity of saying something they think is evident by their deeds.

It's also true that praise can be annoying if it's not sincere, if it's uncreative, if it's the same old thing. Women get tired of being told, "Great meal, honey," if that's all they ever hear in the way of praise. Men don't like being told, "You're so handy," when they really want to be reassured that they're physically attractive.

Insincere praise—which I call flattery and which I'll take up in detail in chapter 5—undermines the whole value of praise.

And nobody likes to be affirmed in a manipulative way. Typically, men suddenly find their wives beautiful when they want to have sex with them; women admire their husbands' skill when they have a list of home projects they want accomplished.

Praise is a tool. There is a right way and a wrong way to use it. We have to learn to use praise well.

ᨦᨦ᠎

One of my worst memories comes from a group exercise that was intended as a feast of affirmation. The magazine I worked for had a staff retreat, partly to plan but partly to (theoretically) bring us closer together. One afternoon we sat in a circle and took turns affirming each other.

The first rule of the game was that you couldn't criticize; you could say only positive things. What was there to fear? Plenty, as it turned out.

The staff wasn't very close; that was why we needed this exercise. I felt quite vulnerable waiting to hear what my peers would say about me.

We went around the circle. All ten or twelve members said a positive word about me. All of them said approximately the same thing. They said that I was smart. Of course, they used different terminology, but that was what it came down to for me. They admired my high IQ.

I didn't want to hear that. I knew I was smart. I had never suffered a moment's doubt about that. What I needed to hear was that I was liked (or loved) for other reasons. Anything would have sufficed, I think: that they liked my smile, that they enjoyed my sense of humor, that my faith in God inspired them. I'd never felt that these people I worked with liked me very much, and after that feast of affirmation I felt it even less. I withdrew. I moped. I kept a stony silence the rest of the retreat. I wasn't courageous enough to tell anyone how I felt. (There was no one whom I trusted that much.) For me it was a thoroughly miserable weekend.

That's extreme, but it shows that praise isn't an all-purpose cure. You have to know the person you're praising. You have to tune in to their needs, their vulnerabilities, their feelings. For a lot of people, being admired for their brains would have been the highest compliment possible. It would have bolstered their confidence for weeks. That didn't include me, though, and if my coworkers had tuned in to that fact, their praise would have been more effective.

∞∞

We sometimes talk as though a person's self-esteem were a helium balloon. We pump a little more gas into it, and it goes higher. Some gas leaks out, and it sinks to earth.

A stool is a better image. Our self-esteem should be a solid platform we can rest our weight on. But if one leg is weak or wobbly, the stool isn't secure, no matter how strong the other legs may be.

I'd identify the four legs of our self-esteem as mental, social, physical, and spiritual. People need to feel capable mentally—to feel that they're sharp enough to get the job done. People need encouragement socially—to know that people like them. They need physical self-esteem—to know that they are attractive. And they need to feel confident spiritually—to know that they are forgiven by God and are in a vital relationship with him.

All four areas need the strengthening we give through praise. If one of these is missing, our platform tips over when we try to stand on it.

Consider, for instance, a very beautiful girl. She knows that people consider her lovely, because she's been told so all her life and because of the way boys follow her with their eyes. To other girls, who want to be beautiful, this girl should be the happiest, most confident female alive. She isn't, however. She is plagued by guilt. Why? Because when she was very small, her parents divorced, and she concluded—as little children often do—that it was her fault. She prayed to God to bring her parents back together, but they stayed apart, and she concluded that God was punishing her by not listening to her prayers.

You can praise that girl all day for her beautiful appearance, but you will do absolutely nothing to help her self-esteem. She needs encouragement spiritually. She needs not only to hear and understand God's grace but to feel it through the grace of another person.

A girl may know that she is very beautiful, but when she feels riddled with guilt, her self-esteem is poor. A boy may have a million friends because of his sense of humor, but when he feels physically ugly, he doesn't have a secure platform to stand on. A woman may know that her husband admires her spiritual life, but when she feels that he doesn't enjoy her company, she is sure to be troubled and nervous in her relations with him.

When I was at the staff retreat, the weak leg of my self-esteem was social. I felt respected, but I didn't feel liked. That weak leg collapsed, and my platform went out from under me.

When you set out to praise someone, it is a good idea to ask yourself: in what area of his or her life is affirmation needed? Often we get locked into one area of affirmation, when what the person needs is something quite different.

Within these four areas—mental, social, physical, and spiritual—you can use tremendous creativity. Just to give you ideas, let me offer examples:

Praise in the mental area

"I like the way you think!"

"It's just amazing the way you keep track of schedules."

"You ask good questions."

"You have such great insight into people (children, our parents, troubled individuals)."

"Thank you for the careful way you balance the checkbook every month."

"You are very helpful when I need to talk through my problems. Thank you for your good questions and insights."

"You are really smart!"

"You are so good at answering the kids' questions."

"You're deep. I appreciate how you ponder things."

"I'm amazed. You always understand how things work."

"How do you know so much? You can converse on a million topics."

Praise in the social area

"You're a wonderful listener."

"I enjoy listening to your friendliness on the phone."

"You care so much for our friends."

"I like how you reach out to strangers. You're very friendly!"

"People really like you when they get to know you."

"You mean so much to me."

"Thank you for being such a good friend."

"I enjoy talking to you."

"You have such deep relationships."

"You have a very comforting presence."

Praise in the physical area

"You're very strong."

"I like looking at you."

"You look very handsome in those clothes."

"It's nice to cuddle with you."

"You have wonderful eyes (skin, hair, feet, nose, teeth, mouth, hands)."

"You're so athletic."

"I find you very attractive."

"You have a beautiful smile."

"You turn me on."

"I like watching you move."

Praise in the spiritual area

"I'm grateful for your steadiness in following God."

"You're a model of someone who understands forgiveness."

"You are such an encourager. You help me want to seek after God."

"Thank you for your integrity. I know I can trust you."

"The consistent way you read the Bible and pray is an example for me."

"People look up to you, do you know that?"

"I like being in Bible studies with you. You have such great insights."

"I can see that God is changing you."

"I'm glad that you are so quick to take concerns to prayer."

"You're really persistent in seeking out the fellowship of Christians. I admire that."

∞∘∾

People also need affirmation in both being and doing. Ask yourself: with the friends and family who matter most, do you praise what they do? Do you praise their being?

Doing

"Thank you for taking the kids out to play football. It's wonderful how you play with them."

"I loved that meal!"

"I am so proud of you for getting that promotion. You are one hard worker!"

"Thanks for making the bed each day. You do so many little things without grumbling or complaining."

"I appreciate you doing all those errands."

Here are a few areas of "doing" that sometimes get overlooked when we praise those we love:

Career
Social Skills
Friendship
Marriage Partner
Lover
Parent
Son or Daughter
Financial Providing
Organization and Planning
Gardening
Housekeeping
Decorating
Sense of Humor
Athletic Ability
Musical Talent/Taste
Home Repairs

Being

It's harder to find ways of admiring someone's being. But people need that kind of affirmation too. They need to know they're admired not just for performing but for being themselves:

"I like living life with you."

"You're a very interesting person, do you know that?"

" I like the way you think."

"You are so masculine [feminine]!"

"I'm so glad that you're a girl [boy]!"

"You know, deep down I trust you. You have real character."

"You're my very favorite three-year-old [seventeen-year-old, fifty-year-old] in the whole world."

"When I'm with you, I feel I can truly be myself."

⤬

You have to plan to use praise. One way is with—again—a piece of paper. Here's a format you can follow to evaluate the way you praise and to plan ways to improve your praising. Follow this format on a separate sheet of paper for each of the important people in your life. Write the actual words—as close as you can come—to affirmations you make. Then think of more and better words to use. It's important to write the actual words you would say, rather than merely the area you'd like to praise. Writing the words is one step closer to actually saying them.

The name of the person who matters to me _____

	How I'm praising now	How I'd like to praise
Mental		
Physical		
Social		
Spiritual		
Doing		
Being		

∽○∽

To become skillful in using this tool of praise, you must become a student of the person you want to encourage. You can't just pick out compliments like flowers—not if you want to use praise to the greatest advantage. You must study those you want to praise, to discover what in their lives deserves praise and where they need strengthening or encouragement. Husbands must become students of their wives. Parents must become students of their children. Friends must become students of their friends, church members of their pastors, bosses of their employees, colleagues of their colleagues.

How do you become a good student? First, as every elementary schoolteacher knows, students must pay attention. When children are talking or passing notes or throwing spit wads, they cannot attend to the subject matter, and they will not learn. Do you really attend to the people in your life? Many wives stopped paying attention to their husbands years ago. Grown children often think of their parents exactly the way they did ten years ago. Friends may completely miss seeing a friend's depression. They simply don't attend. They have their minds on something else.

When I see my parents, I try to read their faces and body language. They usually won't say when they're feeling rotten, but when I pay attention, I can often see it in their eyes. That's an important cue as to what kind of talk will be helpful.

A second important quality for students is motivation. It helps to be smart, but trying hard is even more significant. Many a brilliant mind has underachieved, but students who work hard nearly always "get it" sooner or later. This quality is closely linked to paying attention, because when you really care, you pay attention. This poses a question for us all: how much do we care about the people in our lives? Certainly we would like to get along better, to avoid unpleasant quarrels. But will we work hard to improve? Are we motivated?

One sign of motivation is thinking ahead. I know I'll see my sister this weekend. I know a little bit about the issues she and her family are confronting. Do I care enough to think about what I want to communicate to her? Will I take the time to think of some actual words I'd like to use?

A third important quality for students: good study habits. Most good students take notes. They refer to them for review. Most good students seek out good teachers. They find out who has a good reputation, and they make sure they get into his or her class. If you are to become a student of someone in your life, you may need to jot down your thoughts and observations, perhaps in a journal. Then look back at them from time to time, to review what you've learned. (It's amazing how we forget the most obvious things about each other.) You may also want to seek the insight of someone else who knows the subject well—a "teacher" who can help you understand your subject. My best teacher is my wife. We spend plenty of time talking about our children, our friends, our family members. It's not gossip. It's a serious discussion meant to lead to action.

Fourth, good students stick to it. They don't work hard the first two weeks of class and then forget to study after that. They keep up their study week in, week out.

Many people, however, stop studying those dearest to them. They get a preliminary understanding early on and then stop increasing their knowledge. But people are very complicated, and there's always more to learn. Furthermore, people are always changing. If you're not studying them, you may not notice they have become quite different than they were years—or even months—before.

Just last weekend I saw an old, dear friend. Fred has always been a rough-edged character, a country boy who likes barnyard humor and can put off some people with his bluntness. We don't see each other often now, as we live at opposite ends of the country. During our visit I fell into our old, habitual ways of relating. But after he had gone, I realized that Fred has really changed. There's a softness and a maturity in him that I hadn't seen before. Too bad I kicked back and didn't study on the weekend. I missed a chance to affirm him. I missed a chance to strengthen our friendship.

Fifth, good students ask questions. Their ears are attuned to everything they hear in class, and they aren't afraid to ask questions if they don't understand. It's a talent we all could improve on: listening carefully—to that coworker, that child, that friend—and then asking questions to understand them better. When was the last time you asked your spouse, friend, or parent a question, just seeking to understand them and their needs better?

∽∽∘∽

Here's an exercise you can do on paper. I've used it in conferences for husbands and wives, but it would help almost any relationship where two people are close enough to risk the vulnerability involved.

Sit together with your partner, each of you having paper and a pencil. Silently answer these four questions. Then share your answers with your partner.

1. Describe at least three areas where you feel vulnerable

and would like more affirmation. (It may help to
think of mental, social, physical, and spiritual cate-
gories, or simply of being and doing.)

2. Are there any areas in your life where you feel quite
confident and really don't want or need affirmation
right now?

3. Why is affirming hard for you to do?

4. How could your partner make it easier for you to
affirm him or her?

∽ο∽

Charlie Brown's mother sent notes in his lunch box. This
wonderful idea needn't be restricted to children. Praise need
not only be verbal. How about notes in a purse or wallet?
Notes on the steering wheel? Notes on the desk? Notes
inside the cooking pot? Notes on a bathroom mirror (in lip-
stick)?

Love letters have a fabulous history. They're usually
saved and savored, read again and again. How about a love
letter to your parents? Grown children? Brothers or sisters?
Friends?

Then, for fun, there are always billboards, newspaper
personal ads, skywriting.

I like to think of praise as divided between daily fare and
feasts.

That's the way we eat. Every day isn't Thanksgiving, or
we'd all weigh three hundred pounds. We eat modest, nour-
ishing meals day by day. Every so often we cook a feast. Certain regular traditions require it, like Thanksgiving. But
sometimes we just do it for fun, too.

We worship in the same way. There's the modest fare of

daily prayer and Scripture, the nourishing diet of weekly ser-vices. But occasionally we throw an extravaganza of wor-ship, Christmas and Easter being outstanding examples. Every day can't be Easter. But we need an Easter once a year. Praise is the same. Every relationship needs daily, nour-ishing affirmation: the passing comment, the quick smile and thank you, the word of appreciation. Every so often, however, we need a special celebration of appreciation. That's when we write love letters, make speeches, or call the skywriting company.

∽∾∾

Sometimes people won't accept praise. They may show their discomfort through obvious body language: scowling, look-ing away. They may immediately disagree with what you've said. They may try hard to change the subject. They may make a pious remark about all the credit belonging to God.

If you—like me—find it difficult to praise, this kind of resistance may be quite enough to kill your impulse to affirm. What do you do?

If you know someone who won't accept praise, sit him down and tell him how you feel. Most people are only aware of how uncomfortable *they* feel when someone sings their praises. They haven't thought about how uncomfortable they make *other* people feel by refusing to accept their words. Tell them they're hurting your feelings by discounting what you say. Urge them to:

1. Look you in the eye.
2. Avoid responding negatively or discounting what you say.
3. Say thank you.

You may find it difficult to be so confrontational. However, you're doing a great favor for the person you confront. If you're finding it difficult to break through with praise, other people undoubtedly are having the same experience. Surely your friend (spouse, child, coworker, or parent) puts off their affirmation as well, not just yours. The sooner he or she begins to accept praise, the sooner it can begin to make a difference.

Some people tend to undermine their own words when they affirm. For example:

"That is a beautiful dress. I just wish you'd do something about your hair!"

"I'm so proud that you got an A in math. Now if we could just do something about English!"

Some people seem to have a mechanism inside that balances praise with criticism. It's as though they can't bear to let the person hear only praise! They have to show that they're being fair!

If you catch yourself doing that, make yourself stop it. When you balance praise with criticism, you're not balancing at all. One critical remark weighs ten times as much as one compliment. You're undermining your praise and undoing all the good it can do.

∞

A few days ago a friend said to me, "I'm not good at compliments. I just assume people already know how I feel."

I know that feeling. I could have said those words myself at one time.

Certainly, some people find it hard to praise others. If they are naturally quiet or shy, it's difficult to open up with their feelings. Their style may never be very effusive. It's just not them.

If my friend had been saying, "For me praise is hard work," I would have understood. That wasn't what he meant, however. He meant that he didn't give compliments. They just weren't in his nature.

What he was really implying, I believe, is that praise is optional—a matter of taste. With that I disagree strongly.

I know he would not have said, "I'm just not good at paying my mortgage." If you think something is important, you find a way to get it done.

My deep conviction is that praise is not really optional—not if you truly care about your friends and family. Whatever your personality, you can find a way to get it done. Quiet people can be very effective in praise. When they speak, others sense the significance of their words. A few words of praise from them can accomplish a great deal.

You were created to praise God. When you praise his creatures, you are doing just that. Whoever you are, you can learn to do it. The great question is: are you willing to become that kind of person?

CHAPTER FIVE

Conversational Junk Food: Flattery, Bragging, and Gossip

When words are many, sin is not absent,
but he who holds his tongue is wise.

(Proverbs 10:19)

∽◦∾

Certain ways of talking seem innocent, even pleasant. They bring small but distinctive pleasure to the person speaking. They are like potato chips, tangy and light. One or two are delightful and apparently harmless.

But not many people can stop at one or two. Conversational junk food is addictive. Not only does it cause problems directly—the equivalent of too much salt and fat in the diet—but it crowds out more healthful foods. People eat too many chips, not enough broccoli. Some people's conversations get filled up with flattery, bragging, and gossip. It makes a lousy diet.

Poor nutrition can undermine your health without your realizing it. Similarly, conversational junk food doesn't seem terribly troublesome. Unlike toxic talk it won't leave lifelong scars. It goes scarcely noticed and quickly forgotten.

Yet it hurts. Flattery hurts by undermining real praise. Bragging pushes people away into the outer orbit of your life. Gossip stirs up quarrels and makes the most of differences. Put them together, and you have a portrait of words that hurt.

∽o∾

Flattery

Whoever flatters his neighbor
is spreading a net for his feet.

(Proverbs 29:5)

The extended family I grew up in—farmers, missionaries, housewives, teachers, carpenters—were kindly but never flowery in their language. They rarely gave compliments. I never knew one who could be said to gush.

When I married into a well-off Southern family, it was the verbal equivalent of moving from stony New England to a tropical beach. So warm! So lush! Everybody said nice things. It made me blush, the words people said to me at the elegant parties I attended. With these people, I felt witty and wonderful. I felt like a star coming backstage after a successful show: "They loved me! They *loved* me!"

Over the next several years, however, I began to see another side to this tropical environment. I still liked the way people talked—they had charm and a social grace that was undeniable—but I saw that some people didn't always mean what they said. I heard people saying remarkably warm words to people I knew they quite disliked. At times it was almost a contest to see who could be the most charming. Nobody was expected to take such compliments seriously.

It took me some time, but I eventually put it together. This was flattery! I had heard about flattery but had never really witnessed it. I saw how beguiling it can be. I also saw how dangerous.

⤸⤸

Flattery, in my experience, is most common among wealthy and sophisticated people. Country folks don't flatter; it's the people driving Mercedes who tell each other they look wonderful. They intend to make each other feel good. And they do!

Flattery, I imagine, gets started after someone notices that affirmation is a wonderful thing. When you praise people, they brighten up, feel more confident, relax, and become more effective. So it's good for parents to praise their children. It's good for friends to tell each other why they appreciate each other. It's good for coworkers to admire each other's clothes, hairdo, style. Affirmation is a powerful form of speech.

So the more the better, right? When some people realize how praise can pick up the mood, they want to load it on. If one compliment makes someone's day, two could do more. It doesn't even seem to matter whether the compliment is truthful. If you tell a friend she has lost weight, she feels better even if she knows she hasn't. So why worry about being accurate or sincere? Say nice things, and people will feel better! They'll like you because you make them feel better! That's the idea behind flattery. In the short run it works. In the long run it is a destructive habit of speech.

⤱⤲

Flattery is not just something people do at parties. Flattery has insinuated itself into other situations. For example, it's become a common way of talking to children. It's called "building self-esteem." In recent years, with the psychological realization that a child's self-esteem needs bolstering, there's been an explosion of counterfeit praise, stimulating big growth for the people who manufacture stickers and stamps that say "Terrific!" or "You're a star!"

Once, a sticker from a teacher was a treasure. Nowadays I can discern no pleasure at all in my children when their teacher puts a sticker on their homework. They've had stickers by the hundreds, and they know they don't have to do anything special to get one.

Same with trophies. When I was a young wanna-be athlete, I hardly dared think I could ever earn one. When I won a tiny second-place trophy at a high school tennis meet, it became one of my most prized possessions. Today most kids of my acquaintance have more and bigger trophies by the time they enter the third grade. They get them merely for participating.

I have nothing against freely handing out stickers and trophies, except that I fear the practice may inadvertently rob us of one way of building self-esteem: handing out stickers and trophies. If everyone gets one, they mean nothing, and the kids know it.

More troubling to me, however, is when words of praise are handed out like stickers. To keep their meaning, words of praise need to be specific, thoughtful, and heartfelt.

I am a strong believer in the importance of praising children. It's really not that hard to find something specific and significant to praise in any child. While coaching baseball and soccer I've seen all kinds of kids with all levels of ability, but I've never found it hard to say something genuinely positive about each kid at the end-of-season pizza party. Nor have I found it hard to spot during practice a play, an attitude, or an approach that's praiseworthy. Every kid I coach gets praised regularly, but always for something—however small—that I sincerely appreciated.

I don't say "You're a terrific athlete" when he's not or "Great hustle" when she didn't. I don't try to convince my team that they're all of equally wonderful ability or that the pleasure of their company inevitably thrills me. That would be flattery. Kids are keen at spotting it. If I flattered kids, the result would be subtly but fundamentally destructive: They wouldn't believe my words. They might like me, but I'd have no credibility. My words of praise wouldn't mean anything to them.

Flattery gets you nowhere, because it devalues the currency of praise. The more you flatter, the less people believe you—even when you tell the truth.

∞

Flattery is present even in church when religious people try to flatter God. It starts in exactly the same way as ordinary flattery. Somebody notices that, in a worship service or even in their private prayers, praise is a powerful booster. So they make a rule: Don't start a prayer by asking God for this and that. Start with praise. Tell God how you love him. Tell him how majestic, marvelous, loving and merciful he is.

It is a good rule, and it works. Whether or not praise makes God feel better, it certainly makes the worshiper feel better. The worship service is lifted on wings of praise toward God. People leave church encouraged.

So why not praise more? If some praise is good, more praise will be better, right? Load it on! This may be why some people you meet say "Praise the Lord" at the end of every sentence, like a hiccup. This may be why certain televangelists breathe "Thank you Jesus, thank you thank you Jesus" every time they begin to pray. This may be why the praise portion of some church services becomes such an everlasting ordeal.

I believe strongly that praise is essential to worship—that praise is, in fact, every Christian's first calling. But a percentage of this "praise," I would judge, is mere flattery. It's not false, it's just thoughtless. It's cranked out the way some Southern belles crank out compliments. It's really rather impersonal. Praise isn't given to express deep gratefulness to God; it's given to produce certain emotions in the worshipers. It feels good.

The harm done is the same as when we thoughtlessly praise children: our words lose meaning. If we moan "Thank you Jesus, thank you thank you Jesus" at the launching of every prayer, what do we say when our hearts are truly flooded with thanks? With God too the currency of praise can be devalued by flattery.

∞

"Whoever flatters his neighbor is spreading a net for his feet," Proverbs 29:5 says. Whether flatterers intend it or not, they set people up for failure.

I know a young woman who came out of school with great dreams of her future in publishing. She'd gone to a small college where she was editor of the school newspaper. She'd been a big fish in a small pond, and she didn't realize how small the pond had been. Evidently, she'd heard nothing but admiration from her peers. Faculty members encouraged her to dream big. She was just naïve enough to believe it all.

Actually, she did have ability. But somehow she had gotten through college without any perspective on it. When she hit the competitive world of publishing, it was like a plunge into ice water.

At first she was shocked, then confused, then angry, then deeply discouraged. She simply did not know what to do about the roadblocks she faced. What could she do with her dreams? It was years before she was able to begin the process of accurately evaluating her gifts and redirecting her career. The process was emotionally difficult, because she'd been flattered into thinking that the world was a big apple pie just waiting to be gobbled! Instead she was nearly gobbled herself.

I believe her teachers did her no favor. She deserved, as part of her education, a realistic sense of her strengths and weaknesses—especially at a small college, where the faculty knew her well. They didn't need to squelch her dreams, but they could certainly have given her a more realistic sense of what those dreams required. Instead they egged her on— and she got egg on her face.

Another case: I know a man who sincerely felt a very strong call from God to full-time Christian ministry. He decided to go to seminary to train as a pastor. He was not a good student, and the course work and expense put a great strain on him and his family. But he persevered and got his degree. He then found out what anyone who really knew him might have predicted: that no church, however small and struggling, would call him to be their pastor.

He was a wonderful fellow with a great heart, but he utterly lacked the kind of leadership ability that most churches look for in a pastor. He was mentally disorganized, an enthusiastic but poor speaker; when he led any meeting, he made people feel nervous within ten minutes. Nobody had told him. Instead they had spoken warmly about his calling and had pretended to be delighted at his direction.

They flattered him. I feel quite sure that in private, away from his ears, people discussed his case—but they were never frank with him. He might have been steered into another kind of ministry for which he was admirably suited, but nobody wanted to pop his bubble. Instead they set "a net for his feet."

In the end he was devastated. He had spent years of his life, going in a direction that was from the beginning almost bound to be fruitless.

∽o∽

It is quite a step to actively discourage someone from their dreams. I for one don't want to live in an environment where people constantly pop each other's bubbles. People should take such a step only when they have a relationship of trust or accountability and when they are quite sure of their judgment. It's not a role for everybody.

But we all have a responsibility not to flatter. We should look to encourage people and praise people for specific qualities we truly admire, not to insincerely flatter people for qualities that we truly don't.

It's most crucial in raising children. In my own kids I want to create a realistic, humble self-assessment. I want them to be thankful for their strengths and wary of their weaknesses. I want them to be the kind of people who take a rebuke or a compliment seriously and know how to evaluate whether it's accurate or not. I want them to be unsurprised by struggle and even failure—and also unsurprised by success. I want them to grow up confident but not vain or naïve or stuck on themselves. None of this can happen if I flatter them.

It's the same with my friends. Recently one of them asked me out to lunch. Very emotionally he told me about a painful job evaluation he'd just had. As he talked about it, he grew indignant all over again. His boss had given him an overall mark that he felt was unfair. She had dug up a series of small events from the past year that she felt marked his failure. He felt deeply wounded. He thought about resigning, and he very well might have if he had not had a family to support.

I was glad that he trusted me so much. I certainly hated to see his pain. The easiest thing would have been to share in his outrage over how he'd been treated, to reassure him of his immense talent (to which his boss was blind), and to stoke the fire of his resentment.

I didn't do that. I listened. I sympathized. But I told him that in my experience although job evaluations were often painful, they were also often helpful. I told him that even if his boss was wrong about his performance, he needed to know that his boss *perceived* it as poor. I tried to encourage my friend but also to help him acknowledge that honest people can differ in their assessment of someone's performance.

In short, I did not want to flatter him, nor did I want to eliminate the possibility that he would hear an important correction from his boss. (I don't know whether his boss was right—I don't work with him.) I wanted to stand by him and affirm the strengths that I knew he had. I wanted him to feel my support as his friend. But I also believed the truth—whatever it might be—was ultimately more important than his feelings.

∞∞

Perhaps this example has taken me far away from my starting point. The mindless flattery you hear at a party—"I love your dress!"—is far different from the counsel you give a good friend in distress.

Yet they are related. The habits of the party carry over to the heart-to-heart talk. Flattery over trivial things can and does create an atmosphere where people avoid saying what they truly think, where insincerity is the expected thing. Those beaming compliments, which seem to draw people together by making them feel good, ultimately drive people apart. In the end people stop trusting what others say—stop even paying attention. If you feel obliged to lie about someone's hair, you'll be much more likely to lie about more serious matters that bear the possibility of real pain. If, in my relationship with my friend, we were always buttering each other up, I would have found it hard to have a really candid conversation with him when he was so upset.

If you train yourself to speak sincerely, to never flatter, to encourage truthfully, those habits will carry over throughout your life. They will make you into a different kind of person: someone known for the truth, someone whose encouraging words have meaning, someone to be taken seriously. In the short run, of course, flattery is easier and more gratifying. But in the long run, who do you want to be? Who do your friends and family members want you to be?

∞∞

Bragging

Let another praise you, and not your own mouth;
someone else, and not your own lips.
(Proverbs 27:2)

A second kind of conversational junk food is bragging. It's not a problem for most people, but for the few who tend to brag, it's a *big* problem. Some people seem, judging by the way they talk, to be constantly trying to make an impression. You can't speak with them for five minutes without learning how much they spent remodeling their house, where they went on their fabulous vacation, what great promotion they've accepted, which important people they know, how good an athlete they were in high school, and why all three of their Ivy League–educated children are in line for a Rhodes scholarship.

Bragging is a very specific (and fairly rare) mouth disease. Name-dropping is a variation. A person's level of success seems to have nothing to do with determining who will engage in it. I know people who are very wealthy and fairly famous in their own right yet can't stop dropping names. I also know a man who hasn't held a job for the last ten years yet talks as though he were on the verge of a cabinet appointment. The successful and the unsuccessful brag in the same way. They put people off the same way too.

Bragging is harder to define than flattery. After all, it's important to let friends and family know what's happening in your life. You want to share the honors you've received, the acquisitions that excite you. That's a part of sharing yourself.

Some friends of mine recently added on to their house. It was all they could talk about. Given half a chance, they would provide a tour, proudly showing off the many features of the room they had thought about so long and so hard. It was fun sharing their excitement. They were so evidently pleased!

That's different from bragging. The goal of sharing is to let people know you. The goal of bragging is to make people admire you. Sharing draws people into your experience. Bragging lifts you up above other people's experience. Bragging is essentially antisocial and competitive.

For example, take that well-known figure, the bragging grandmother. Some grandmothers are a delight, because they are genuinely thrilled with their grandchildren, and their excitement bubbles over. You like looking at their pictures (which they pull from their purse at a moment's notice), because it is fun to see someone so terribly pleased with the common miracle of children. And they act quite interested in seeing your pictures as well, or hearing your stories.

Other bragging grandmothers, however, fill you with dread when they dive into their purse. They seem unaware of others; they merely tolerate someone else's pictures, giving them "equal time" only so that they can go back to singing their own song.

Sharing involves give-and-take, listening as well as talking, admiring as well as being admired. Bragging is self-centered. Sharing is sensitive to others' feelings, sympathizing whenever they are accidentally bruised. Bragging is annoyed when other people's sensitivities—the childless couple's sadness, for example—stymie their chance to show off.

The main reason not to brag is simple: people hate it. It will never really help you gain status; it will always push people away. They will joke about you behind your back.

Some braggarts have so many other endearing qualities that friends overlook their name-dropping and bragging. Even so, bragging changes their relationships for the worse.

I have the impression that most braggarts aren't aware of their bragging—or at least aren't aware of how much other people dislike it. If they were aware, surely they would not continue it! But bragging is junk food. You can consume a lot without realizing it.

So ask yourself: What was I sharing when I talked about myself? Was I sharing excitement, pleasure, gratefulness for God's goodness? Or was I really sharing my own importance?

And ask yourself: How did I affect others? Did I draw people into my joy, or did I set myself apart? In what direction did I expect this conversation to take me—closer to other people or higher above the crowd?

If you're at all unsure about this evaluation, get some help. A spouse, a close friend, or a trusted counselor should be able to tell you the truth as others see it.

If you tend to brag, you would be better to close your mouth and keep quiet. Better yet, though, would be to learn how to share in a way that's generous to your friends, makes them feel they are a part of your life, and is sensitive to their peculiar vulnerabilities. Braggarts put the spotlight on themselves. If you share yourself while thinking of others, you will become a very different kind of person.

∽∞∾

Gossip

> Without wood a fire goes out;
> without gossip a quarrel dies down.
>
> *(Proverbs 26:20)*

Gossip is the most popular of all the conversational junk food. It is potato chips and soda put together. If all gossip in the world were to one day suddenly cease, a stunned silence would follow. Much of what passes for active, witty conversation is typically gossip. People who like to talk—and I am one of them—find it hard to quit.

As with bragging, gossip is hard to define exactly. Certainly, you know when you've been around gossip, but whether a particular statement is gossip can be hard to determine. Somebody says that his friend Mark is putting a second story on his house. Is that gossip? Somebody else mentions that Bob and Susan are going out, that they're serious. Is that gossip or just the healthy sharing of friends?

Mere information shades gradually into sheer gossip. There's room for disagreement as to whether a particular statement is gossip or not.

Just the other night, my family was discussing a problem at our church: a lack of discipline in the youth group. My daughter, who is sensitive to these things, suddenly said that she didn't want to discuss it any further; she felt we were gossiping.

I didn't. It seemed to me that we were discussing an issue of importance to us and weren't undercutting any of the people involved. I said so, but Katie was politely adamant. She just wouldn't talk about the subject anymore, so we had to move on to something else.

Thinking it over later on, I had to admire her discernment. Talking about our church youth group isn't necessarily gossip, but we had subtly turned a corner. We were beginning to enjoy its problems. We had moved from soberly considering a course of action to finding a perverse enjoyment in somebody else's dilemma. The conversation had stopped doing any good and had started doing harm. What harm? We will look at that in more detail shortly. But I will now say at least this: while we were discussing the youth group's problems we weren't talking about other subjects that could have encouraged us, helped us, lifted us up. Junk food conversation was crowding out healthier foods.

∽∘∾

How to define gossip? You can't precisely. But you can identify gossip fairly accurately by the following characteristics:

Gossip prefers bad news to good. I don't hear people buzzing about the news that someone's daughter is valedictorian at her high school. I hear them buzzing that someone's daughter got picked up by the police.

Because of this preference for bad news, gossip often isn't very accurate. It often makes things sound worse than they really are.

Consider that girl who got picked up by the police. News may quickly spread that, according to a classmate at school, she has been running with gang members. The fact that the girl claims it was a case of mistaken identity on the part of the police might not even get mentioned. When that turns out to be basically true—and all charges are dropped—the phone lines will not be nearly so busy. Some people may never even hear the end to the story—that there was no problem after all. Gossip has a bias toward scandal.

In 1 Corinthians 13:7 Paul writes that love "always trusts, always hopes. . . ." Gossip, on the other hand, always suspects, always expects . . . the worst.

"Without wood a fire goes out," says Proverbs 26:20, "without gossip a quarrel dies down." When two people or two groups are at odds, gossip keeps reminding both sides of their problems. Gossip doesn't bring a balanced perspective or a reminder of the other side's good qualities. It feeds the quarrel with bite-sized reminders of bad qualities, bad decisions, bad reputations. Quarrels otherwise tend to wind down, because people get distracted and have other concerns to worry about. Gossip keeps them stoked up.

Gossip takes *pleasure* in other people's problems. This is closely related to my previous point. Talking about others' troubles isn't always wrong, of course. But gossip always turns the corner toward *enjoying* someone else's misfortune.

Often this enjoyment comes under the guise of wanting to help. That's why "prayer requests" are a terrific way to gossip. I remember some years ago when a young couple in our church split up. It was a horrible, gut-wrenching experience for everyone who knew them. As word of their separation spread, many people were moved to pray for them, to talk to them, to offer practical assistance to the partner left with small children.

Before long, however, the urgent phone calls should have stopped. Those who were in a position to help them or talk to them were already doing so. The rest of us didn't need an update on their latest fruitless effort at reconciliation. We didn't need to know that divorce papers had been filed. We merely needed to know what we already did know: that they were in trouble and needed our prayers.

It wasn't the pleasure of helping two struggling people that kept the phone lines busy. Sure, there was genuine concern for them and their children. Increasingly, though, it was the pleasure of being in the know about other people's problems.

Gossip spreads intimate information. One way to test whether you're gossiping is to ask: how would they like hearing us talk about them this way? Would they feel that we really cared? Or would they feel that we were trading information about them like vendors at a swap meet?

People differ in their concern for confidentiality. Some don't care who knows about their personal lives, while others feel violated if even the most trivial detail of their life has been spread around. Unless you know, the best rule is to assume complete confidentiality.

I happen to be someone who doesn't feel strongly about "personal" information being spread around. If I tell one friend about something I'm struggling with, it doesn't bother me that other friends might find out. Not everyone feels that way, though, and I've come to understand their sensitivity. When people trade inside information about their friends, it can become a commodity and cheapen the relationship.

Celebrities experience this cheapening most dramatically. News about their personal affairs gets written into gossip columns, fan magazines, and tabloids. Juicy tidbits are literally worth money to someone willing to sell them to the media.

Celebrities generally feel this is a loss of their privacy, and it is. They become less friendly to strangers and acquaintances. They build strong fences and hire bodyguards to keep their private lives from being overrun.

That's the extreme, but it illustrates the impact of gossip. Even when news isn't scandalous, it needs to be handled with a genuine sensitivity to the feelings of the person involved. If he or she would feel uncomfortable overhearing you blab about his or her personal life, you'd better not do it. It's gossip.

I once helped Dave Dravecky, the baseball player, write a book about his battle to make a comeback from cancer.

Dave and his wife, Janice, are wonderfully open people. They don't hide their struggles; they talk openly about their marital difficulties, for example. They even went on to write about them in another book.

When I was working with them, they were at a celebrity peak. I met people everywhere who wanted to know how the Draveckys were doing. I am sure Dave and Janice would have told them plenty if they had been asked directly. They weren't keeping secrets. Nevertheless, I didn't tell curious people much about the Draveckys' struggles, even though I was tempted to. I could have done it under the pious cover of encouraging people to pray for the Draveckys. It felt good to be in the know about such fine and celebrated people; it would have felt even better to talk and let others know how much I knew. But in doing so I would have cheapened their lives and our relationship. I would have been using them and their intimate affairs for no good purpose other than making myself seem more important. That's gossip.

∽∽

There's one test for gossip that applies to all junk food conversation: Does it nourish the soul? You can't define gossip precisely, and some conversations will always be in doubt. But conversations that really nourish generally focus on the personal concerns of you and me. Gossip always concerns somebody else.

Maybe the worst aspect of gossip is that it fills time and keeps us from talking intimately about ourselves, about our own troubles and woes and joys. Gossip keeps us chatting about other people and avoiding the more personal probing that would bring us closer together. Nobody walks away from gossip feeling warm or tearful. Nobody walks away feeling glad they made themselves vulnerable and gained a closer friend. Gossip is junk food, and it leaves a residue of dissatisfaction. The soul needs food, and gossip fills it up with something else.

I said that if all gossip stopped, there would be a long silence. But the silence would eventually be filled with something else, perhaps something better. Eliminating gossip from your conversation can make you a different person by making space for a better way of talking.

CHAPTER SIX

Talking about Trouble

Wounds from a friend can be trusted,
but an enemy multiplies kisses.

(Proverbs 27:6)

How I wish all our words could be positive! But real life includes problems, and effective speech confronts those problems.

I am thinking of two brothers. Years ago when they were children, the older brother took to ridiculing the younger one. He made fun of his brother's involvement in the church choir, which he knew meant a great deal to his brother. He would tease until his brother began to cry, and then he would ridicule his brother even more for being a crybaby. Why their parents let this go on I don't know. But they did.

That was more than twenty years ago. Both brothers are too grown up to act so mean now, but their attitudes—contempt on one side, bitterness on the other—haven't changed very much. They see each other at family reunions, funerals, and weddings. They act as though all is well. They even hug each other. But it's a chilly relationship. Unresolved anger keeps them from ever becoming close. And neither one will take the first step toward talking it out.

I wonder how many relationships are like that. How many husbands and wives harbor unforgiven grudges or resentments? How many brothers and sisters, parents and children, old friends, neighbors, and workmates act as though everything is normal when in fact it isn't?

In those situations the most beautiful words that can come from your mouth are those that begin talking about the trouble. Avoiding an argument when you can is right. But avoiding a confrontation at all costs isn't. In fact, at the right time and in the right way people should seek confrontation. Life isn't all sunshine. People must deal with the darkness.

~~o~~

If people won't confront trouble, their talk inevitably becomes shallow. You meet people who have made avoidance a lifestyle. They may be cheerful, eloquent, and likable, but somehow there's a vagueness between them and their family and friends, because they won't deal with hard personal issues. When difficulties come up, they change the subject.

I'm thinking of a man who always tells a joke when you try to have a serious discussion. I'm thinking of a woman who, when you try to sit down for a heart-to-heart talk, invariably has to run somewhere on some errand that can't wait.

It's certainly not easy to talk about trouble. There's always the potential that anger will get out of hand. Hurtful words may be said, and friendships may be broken.

On the other hand, no real relationship goes on without difficulty. Conflict, in fact, shows life. When people face their differences and surmount them, they grow closer.

I've risked talking about trouble many times and with many different friends. In a few cases, at least partly due to my blunders, it has pushed us further apart. More often it has led to greater understanding, with a release of thankful emotions. When you get the hard feelings out, the softer feelings can appear. Talking about trouble is risky, but it can—and does—lead to genuine intimacy. As many couples have found, making up can almost compensate for the pain of fighting.

∽∽o∾∽

Most people, if they're close, have developed a style for handling differences. Here is a short list of approaches people use to deal with issues that really bother them. Do you recognize any that apply to you?

> yelling
> clamming up (the "silent treatment")
> leaving/escaping
> shopping
> reading
> watching TV
> eating
> working long hours
> drinking/taking drugs
> using sarcasm or "humor"
> crying
> depression
> self-pity

No doubt, the list could be longer. My personal approach differs depending on who is involved. When it's trouble with my children, I tend to make long, eloquent speeches, leaving no room for rebuttal. With my wife I usually get moody, silent, and depressed, hoping she'll notice. With those outside my family I've sometimes written long, eloquent letters, again, leaving no room for a rebuttal.

None of these styles is very effective in dealing with trouble, and I sometimes have to spend quite a lot of energy undoing the additional trouble I've created because of my approach.

Someone has suggested that there are five general ways of dealing with difficulties. From worst to best they are:

avoidance
competition
accommodation
compromise
collaboration

Most of the styles I've listed—like yelling, shopping, working long hours—fall under avoidance or competition. They are, I think, the most common ways of talking about trouble: either you *don't* talk or you have it out to see who can pin the other to the mat. Sometimes competition can be subtle. It may involve a son trying to build a bigger house than his father, a husband trying to get more affection from a child than his wife gets, a sister determined to play Monopoly—and win—every time the family is together.

Accommodation is a little better. It occurs when one person simply goes along with the other's wish. Some things aren't worth fighting over, and it's easier just to give in. But please note: accommodation doesn't lead to greater intimacy. Oftentimes it avoids trouble at one point only to meet it again at another. For example, I can go along with my brother's preference for the site of the family reunion. But my resentment may set us up for conflict when the reunion comes.

Compromise is a great improvement—each one giving up some rights to find a place in the middle. But collaboration is the best. Collaboration happens when two or more people manage to see beyond their differences to the goals they share. They find a way to work toward those goals together. It's not exactly the same as compromise, though it often involves compromise. Fundamentally, it requires a new vision of how the two of you can complement each other—how the very differences that separate you can, in fact, begin to work together for the common good. True collaboration usually comes only after a lot of communication and a lot of emotion.

My wife and I have had different visions about the place of baseball in our lives. I love it—in fact, I have been accused of being addicted to it. She resents baseball. She can't even stand the sound of a game on the radio, because it "takes over." We have had more than a few conflicts based on this over the years. Collaboration began to occur between us, however, when she made up her mind to appreciate the hours I spend practicing baseball with my sons, and I agreed to drop out of the church softball team to leave more time for other activities. Those were compromises, but compromises based on a shared vision of how baseball best benefits our family. Before, it was just "I love baseball; you resent it." It took some work to find a perspective we could share. It's not perfect, and it will probably take more work— but at least we're working together. We never could have if we hadn't tried, repeatedly, to talk about the issue.

∞o∞

You have to start somewhere. Sometime, somewhere, somebody has to take a deep breath and say, "There's something I need to talk to you about." The problem is, how do you determine if this is the time to raise the issue? And if now is the time, just exactly where do you begin?

Here are three guidelines to consider before you take the plunge:

1. Talk about trouble if you're the only one who can (perhaps because you're the only one who knows what's wrong). Sometimes, like the prophet Nathan, who confronted King David, you have to go talk to someone simply because no one else will. You don't want to gossip about the problem. If no one else can or will bring it up directly—you're it.

2. Talk about trouble if there's a problem that truly needs fixing. Some "trouble" really comes down to personality or taste. For example, you may consider it a terrible thing that the church building committee has decided to repaint the church beige instead of the traditional white. But do you really need to make a fuss? I'd say no, unless some larger issue—financial dishonesty, for example—is involved. Just because you don't like the color doesn't mean you have to talk to someone about it. Part of living in community with other people is eating what's put on your plate. (If you don't like it, volunteer to cook next time.)

3. Talk about trouble if it interferes with a relationship. If that beige paint sticks in your craw so much that your best friend on the building committee is becoming an "ex-friend," you'll need to deal with that. But be clear: the problem you want to solve isn't the paint, it's your feelings.

∾∾∾

If you've decided yes, you really need to talk, the next question is when. The Bible says you should "not let the sun go down on your anger" (Ephesians 4:26)—very good advice, for it allows problems to be dealt with as they come up. If you're angry, deal with your anger within twenty-four hours. Don't store it up for some future date.

Be careful, though. The Bible doesn't say you must solve all your problems within twenty-four hours. Some couples have interpreted this verse in Ephesians to mean that they must achieve complete peace and harmony before they go to bed. I did this myself when newly married. "We're not going to sleep until we've settled this," I said. But as the hour grew later we both grew more exhausted, more emotionally distraught, and further from a solution. We only made things worse. Problem-solving after bedtime isn't the best idea for us.

Here's a better way. If you can't settle it now, make an appointment to do it later. Say something like this: "This isn't the best time right now—we're tired, and there's too much going on—but could we set a time to talk about this? I want to make sure we have enough time to really understand each other." Get out your calendars and plan to meet each other when you both are as rested as possible, in a place where you won't be interrupted. That won't settle all the turbulent feelings, but it will probably deal with anger enough so that you both can sleep.

And it will make sure that you really do talk. One of the worst mistakes is to keep putting off the conversation to some unidentified "later." Most people want to run away from the emotional stress of talking about trouble. When you've both said you're going to talk and have put it on your calendar, it's far more likely you really will.

∽০∾

The time of your appointment has come. The answering machine is taking your phone calls; your time is free. You take a deep breath and begin to talk. But where do you start?

Begin with at least three affirmations. You probably want to plunge right into the problem, but take time to spell out a few good things. Affirm your relationship and how much it means to you. (If it doesn't, why are you talking?) Affirm positive qualities that balance the problem you perceive. For instance, if you want to talk about your partner's tendency to overspend, make sure that you affirm that he really brings delight to others with his generous habit of picking up the check. Affirm his basic character—his trustworthiness, his joyfulness, his love for his family.

Affirming accomplishes two things. First, it helps you keep concerns in perspective. There's a problem you need to deal with, but there are many other aspects of your relationship that aren't a problem—in fact, they're good.

Affirming also aids communication. Most people "hear" criticism far more readily than affirmation. That's why you need to make at least three affirming comments for every negative one. If your complaint isn't (over)balanced by affirmation, the person listening will probably get a message of total condemnation and rejection. They'll hear "I hate you, you're worthless, and you've got to change everything about yourself for me to accept you." Obviously, if that's what they hear, they will find it hard to work toward a solution with you.

You always need to affirm when you criticize. You particularly need to do it with someone feeling threatened and vulnerable.

A friend recently came to me distraught. He and his wife weren't speaking. I asked him whether any incident had sparked the feud. "Yes," he said and described how he had raised a troublesome subject with her. He had done it, he said, in the most careful and cautious way he could imagine, but she hadn't spoken to him since.

I knew enough to figure out what had happened. A year ago his wife lost a job from which she drew much of her sense of self-worth. With no visible prospects for employment, she's emotionally very vulnerable. His words, however cautiously expressed, devastated the last shreds of self-respect she was holding on to. If he had to raise the issue at all—it's not quite clear that he did—he needed to work doubly hard to put it into a context of appreciation and admiration.

Be specific about what is troubling you. It may be that what's bothering you is a pattern of behavior or an attitude you perceive. It's hard to discuss an attitude, however. You have to start with specific events. What happened that made you notice this attitude?

Try "It really bothered me last week when the check you wrote to Macy's bounced" instead of "Your carelessness with finances is going to ruin us."

Try "When you asked Robin if she would take on designing that brochure, I felt you were taking over my job as the chair of the committee," not "You undermine everyone to whom you give an assignment."

Try "Twice this week you've left your jacket at school," not "You don't even care about the clothes we buy for you."

Explain how it makes you feel and why it matters to you. You can't be sure of someone else's attitude. But you do know how you feel, and you need to express that. Speak of what you know about yourself.

"When a check bounces, I feel really frustrated because I fear our finances are out of control."

"When you ask somebody to do work that I'm responsible for, I start feeling like you don't trust me."

"When you forget your jacket, I worry that you just don't care and that you're going to have a lot of problems in life when I'm not around to help you out."

Don't rush toward a solution. You may already have an answer all cooked up in your mind, but first say, "This is really bothering me. Do you think we could work together toward a solution?" Make sure you talk the problem out before trying to settle it. Offer your solution by saying, "Do you think this would help?" In other words, try to create an atmosphere of collaboration.

∽०∽

When you've screwed up your courage and raised the difficult subject, your work has just begun. You hope the person you've talked to will thank you for your help and go on to change his behavior. This rarely happens. More often, talking about trouble seems to make trouble worse before making it better. People will sidetrack you by attacking your faults, by making a scene, by bathing in self-pity. When you talk about trouble, you begin a dialogue; you must also be ready to listen.

Whole books have been written on the subject of listening. I find many people are somewhat familiar with the information these books typically offer. That doesn't mean they're *using* it, however. Perhaps this checklist will help you think about how you listen to the response that comes when you talk about trouble.

Concentrate. Listening is active. It requires involvement. Forget about what your response will be. Don't worry about what you'll say next. Listen hard. Try to understand what's being said and the meaning behind it.

Show interest. Look her in the eye while she's talking. Nod. Make encouraging sounds—"Hmmm," "Yes." Don't yawn. Don't look at your watch. Don't frown.

Don't defend yourself right away. Be quick to listen, slow to respond. If a dialogue deteriorates into two people attacking each other, it will go nowhere. At least one of you has to show more interest in finding common ground than in defending yourselves. It may as well be you.

Watch your humor. There is a kind of humor that's helpful—the kind that diffuses tension and makes both of you laugh. The right kind of joke reminds both of you that you really do like each other.

More common, I'm afraid, is barbed humor. I'll give an example. Last night my wife said something she often says when she's discouraged: "I don't feel connected to you."

I responded with a wisecrack. "Gee, it seems to me I've heard this before." I said it in a tone that was meant to be humorous. But Popie didn't think it was funny. She sensed, correctly, that I was annoyed by her comment and was using humor (of a not-very-funny variety) to strike back.

A lot of humor is disguised aggression. Mine was!

Fortunately, Popie was not deterred by that. She let me know that she didn't like my feeble joke, and we were able to talk about the real issue. Instead of joking, I should have asked her to rephrase the problem. When she said she didn't feel connected, she meant to say something I like to hear: that she wanted to spend some time together. I heard something different, though. I heard her accusing me of not paying attention to her. I reacted defensively. When we talked about my reaction, we got somewhere.

Repeat back the meaning—briefly! To show you understand, echo the message in your own words. "You're saying that you really don't bounce many checks." "You're saying that you always feel too hurried at the store to write down how much you have spent."

Ask feeling questions. Detective Sam Slade was famous for saying, "Just the facts, ma'am." That may be a good approach for detective work, but it is a terrible approach for talking about trouble. It's feelings that cause most problems, and those need to be talked through: "How did you feel when I said I was disappointed in you?"

Ask linking questions. Often you gain insight when you put together a pattern of events. Sometimes they aren't at all similar in terms of the facts; they just *feel* the same. "Was this like the time when your boss criticized you for going to the dentist during office hours?" By asking linking questions, you explore the terrain of another person's mind.

Look for root causes. Try to find out what's behind the behavior. For example, a child may be throwing all his papers and clothes in a pile when he comes in the door after school. Maybe it's just thoughtlessness. But maybe it's linked to the great stress he's under during school hours because his best friend just moved away and he feels lost without him. Maybe he's about to explode from the tension by the time he finally arrives at the safety of his home. The lack of friends doesn't excuse the mess, but it helps you understand so you can respond appropriately.

Often undesirable behavior masks the real problem. Dialogue should go beyond the symptoms of behavioral problems to the deeper issues.

Be patient—the world doesn't have to change in one hour. Often you won't settle a problem in one sitting. At least you got started. You've opened up dialogue, and now it can continue.

∽o∽

What hinders listening? What keeps a dialogue from developing when you talk about trouble? Here's a partial list:

Distractions. Most people find it hard to listen when they are interrupted by noise, telephone calls, people coming and going. Try to arrange a quiet, private place to talk.

Preoccupation. You can't really listen while you're thinking about something else. It takes an effort to put other subjects out of your mind and concentrate strictly on what's being said. Sometimes this is not possible. Having grown up as a pastor's son, I know instinctively that it's unwise to try to hold a serious conversation with a minister on Sunday morning. He has too many other things on his mind.

Answering feeling with fact. When someone is expressing his feelings, it's deadly to answer him only with facts. Listen for the feelings, and don't smash them with "proof" that they're wrong. Feelings may be inappropriate or misdirected, but they must be understood. They demand empathy and understanding.

Class or cultural differences. Listeners often miss important cues when they're from a different background. For example, an African psychiatrist told me about his training in England, where he was treating a depressed widower. The psychiatrist couldn't figure out any trigger for the depression until his supervisor pointed out that the widower's pet dog had recently died. It was an obvious cause to another Englishman, but incredible to an African. How could a dog cause depression?

Cultural differences occur between Americans, too. When a neighbor died, my wife and I took our children to the funeral. It was an open-casket service, and we all marched forward to pay our respects—including Silas, who was only a toddler. Afterwards, from the comments of other neighbors, I realized they had been shocked at our including Silas. It so happens that in my family culture dead bodies aren't regarded as fearful for children. I've been raised to believe that viewing the body can help children grasp the reality of death. My neighbors came from a different culture. In some situations—such as between a husband and a wife who are distraught over the death of a loved one—these cultural differences could create deep misunderstandings.

When you're dealing with class or cultural differences, it's often helpful to involve a third party who can act as a translator. Otherwise, try as you may, you may lack important background information.

Weariness, discomfort, or pain. If you are falling asleep or are shivering with cold or have a splitting headache, you might do better to make an appointment for another time.

Trying to come up with a wise-sounding answer (especially while your partner is still talking). Sometimes a good listener won't come up with any answer at all. He'll just listen. That's all that's required.

Lack of time. You can't listen in a hurry. It's hard to do it between appointments. If you want to be the kind of person who can talk about trouble, you will have to make time to do it.

Repetition and verbosity. You've said your piece. You've raised the troubling issue. You usually don't need to repeat it. The more you're talking, the less you're listening.

Insecurity. It's hard to listen calmly when you lack confidence in yourself. Whatever strengthens your sense of security—prayer, the presence of friends, a familiar setting—will help you listen.

∽∘∾

I have mentioned that I tend to write letters to people when something is bothering me. I'm a writer by profession. Naturally, I want to write it out. To me it *feels* like the right thing to do. Working at my computer, I can carefully choose the precise words I want. I don't have to worry about blurting out the wrong thing. Every word can be carefully considered.

There's only one trouble: people misunderstand. They misunderstand what I say, and they misinterpret my motives. What seems to be the ideal way to express my concerns often turns out to be the worst.

I remember writing to my friend Paul, trying to express my deep, caring concern about a relationship he was in. I knew something was wrong when I got his response—a letter that must have weighed half a pound, there were so many pages stuffed inside. On the envelope he had written, "Warning: mad dog inside!" He was furious.

I don't think Paul misunderstood because my letter wasn't well crafted. I think he misunderstood because at some unconscious level he wanted to. It was easier to get mad at me than to deal with the problem I had raised. When we confront others with a problem, their defenses go up. They're primed to misunderstand. At least, that's how *I* am when people bring up sore subjects with me.

That's why I now prefer to talk about trouble in person, not through the mail. Misunderstandings and suspicions are bound to arise when you talk about trouble. In person you can clear them up right away. Through the mail, they may linger and grow for days, even weeks.

I do see one advantage in writing. If a subject is so emotional that you can't express yourself very well, or if you feel the person you're talking to will dominate the conversation and keep you from giving your point of view in full, write out your whole speech. But don't send it. Carry it. Read it out loud, or wait while the person you're confronting reads it to himself. Then you can begin the dialogue.

∽∘∽

When I was in college, I spent a school term living with my older brother and his wife Barbara. Bill was doing graduate studies in New Haven, Connecticut. Barbara was putting him through school while working for the welfare department. I slept on their foldout couch and worked as a busboy. We had a good time together—I thought.

Just before the school term was over, when I was soon due to head back home to California, Barbara brought her gripes to the surface. Without going into detail—I can't even remember the detail—I'll simply say that I'd been taking them for granted financially. I had been contributing to rent, but there were some significant extra expenses that I'd managed not to think about. I had behaved like a typical college student, assuming the world owed me a living. It bugged Barbara, and now she brought it all out.

I was mortified, angered. How could she doubt my motives? I hadn't meant to shortchange them. To me they seemed to have plenty of money. All this and more poured out in emotional dialogue to the background music of my brother holding his head and saying woefully, "Oh, I didn't want this to happen!"

When it was all over, we were fine. In fact, we felt terrific. Barbara had gotten it off her chest. I had said I was sorry. Sometimes talking is all that's needed. Getting it out in the open can relieve sore feelings and make everything all right. I've always been grateful to my sister-in-law for her willingness to talk about the problem. She cleared the air and let us become far closer to each other.

We didn't have to find a long-range solution, because I was leaving. In other cases it's not so simple. After you've aired the problem, you still have to find a way to improve things.

Take family finances—a traditional issue to fight over. You do need to talk long and hard, trying to understand each other's point of view. You have to look for the real issues behind the behavioral problems. For example, if the person who earns the most money seems to have the upper hand in deciding financial questions, it may create resentments and resistances that have nothing to do with sensible budgets.

You may never perfectly agree about family finance, but you have to find some way to manage them. If your current system isn't working, you have to find some other way. Separate checkbooks? Monthly allowances?

However quickly you want to settle it, avoid premature compromises. It's emotionally wearing to talk about trouble, and you usually begin to long for some way to put the issue to bed. One of you may be willing to give in, to compromise for the sake of peace. For example, one of you may agree to go along with very strict budgeting, even though he or she doesn't feel that his or her interests were truly considered in the way the budgets were reached.

That kind of solution isn't a solution at all. Ultimately it will create more problems than it solves. It's better to arrive at no solution than an unstable one. You don't really have to solve the problem in one day. Make an appointment to talk about it more, later. Rather than settling for an inadequate solution, agree to get together again to work at something better. Agree about where to look for help—in books, in friends' advice. Do some research into how other families handle money. Patch together an interim solution, but leave the long-range plan to another time.

When you do agree on a plan—a budget, a way of controlling funds—adopt it on a trial basis: "Let's give this three months, and then review." And again (is this getting familiar?) make an appointment. Set a time to review it, so that you really will. Don't let an inadequate solution continue indefinitely.

Of course, no solution is perfect, because people have different values and different styles. To live together, we have to compromise. For a wife and husband who think in different ways about money, family finances will probably always be a chronic problem. They won't solve it once and for all.

What a difference it will make, however, if they can talk about their trouble. They may not—and probably won't—find a golden budget that removes all their stress. If they can discuss it, though, there will be something golden in their relationship. Airing the problems that come up day by day and learning to understand and sympathize with each other's point of view, will help them become a different kind of people.

∾∾

A final word of warning is needed. If you are going to confront someone—a spouse, a friend, a coworker—you must demonstrate two fundamental commitments. You must show yourself as being committed to the process of dialogue, and you must show yourself as being committed to the relationship.

I remember a girl I knew in college. Susan had fallen in love with a non-Christian and decided to marry him. She was a very strong member of our Christian fellowship group, the other members of which were appalled at her plans. Since the Bible warns against interfaith marriages, they felt that she was throwing herself into sin.

One by one—and two by two—people went to talk Susan out of it, warning her against the consequences of her plans. She listened to each person—she was a lovely and winsome woman—but as more and more came she grew increasingly bitter. Eventually she wanted nothing to do with the fellowship. She ended her years of college estranged from other Christians, an estrangement that continued for many years. Incidentally, she did marry the man she loved; sadly, they were eventually divorced.

Quite possibly Susan would have become estranged from the group no matter how the members confronted her. Nonetheless, the people who went to her made some mistakes. She felt like a target, as if people came to "do their duty" by warning her against sin. Some didn't even know her well. It felt impersonal and uncaring to her—though I am sure they meant to be caring.

The problem, as I see it now, was that too many people tried to talk to her. Only a few needed to—perhaps only two or three. They should have been the people who could best demonstrate their fidelity to these two commitments:

Commitment to the process of dialogue. They needed to demonstrate their willingness to listen long and hard. They needed to show a deep and patient desire to understand how things appeared to Susan—not just to dump a cold message and wait threateningly for the "right" answer. Listening is just as important as speaking. You have to show that you understand this, and that you are committed to it.

Commitment to the relationship. They needed to show Susan they would continue caring for her no matter what she decided. They needed to show themselves as being committed to her regardless of whether they could agree.

Susan didn't feel this from the people who came to talk. They had made up their minds, she felt, and didn't want to listen. Furthermore, many of them never had much of a relationship with her to start with and wouldn't miss her if she went away. They all came across as cold and uncaring.

Such problems aren't restricted to earnest college students. I often see them in struggling married couples. Usually one of the partners is trying desperately to force a resolution to their problems, while the other one won't cooperate. The uncooperative partner may get blamed, but frequently the problem is more complicated than it looks. The uncooperative partner may sense that the other person doesn't really want to understand his or her view, or is not truly committed to the relationship. What if that other partner is merely trying to win a compromise that he will ultimately use against him or her?

To talk about trouble effectively, you must *demonstrate* these commitments. That's more than just saying it. It won't hurt to say it, however—to take time to spell it out—when you bring up a painful subject.

CHAPTER SEVEN

The Right Word at the Right Time

A word aptly spoken
is like apples of gold in settings of silver.

(Proverbs 25:11)

My niece Jenny, who is due to graduate from college this spring, will always be remembered in our family for something she said when she was three years old. Her mother was irritated with her and asked, "Jenny, how would you like something that starts with an S and ends with a K?"

Jenny replied sweetly, "I would rather have something that starts with a K and ends with an S."

When I relate this story, I often have to tell adult listeners that the relevant words are *spank* and *kiss*.

Precocious children are always interesting, especially to their relatives, but Jenny's answer was fascinating for another reason. She made something we dream of: the perfect comeback.

∽∾

Some people are amazingly quick. Their clever responses seem to come faster than the speed of thought. Unfortunately, I am not one of these people, but I do treasure in my memory one time when I came up with just the right thing to say.

Popie and I were speaking at a weekend retreat for young married couples. They were a highly educated group; many of them were making a lot of money, and all were very determined to succeed at their careers. Yuppies, in short. Many were working so hard they had no time or energy left for each other. That was a significant issue in their marriages.

We were speaking after another couple, Gary and Judie Hagen, on Saturday morning. Gary, who is retired from the military, read aloud a letter of appreciation he'd received from his grown son. Gary got very choked up as he read.

Then it was my turn to speak. I walked to the podium feeling that nobody was ready for my message; they were still processing Gary's emotions. How to make the transition?

"I'm fairly sure," I said to the young couples, "that none of us twenty years from now will be standing in front of an audience, choking up as we read over our old paystubs."

There was a roar of laughter, and when it waned, people were ready to listen. The humor moved people from being embarrassed by Gary's emotions to appreciating the reason for them—his deep involvement with his son. It also gently poked fun at their obsession with work. I had said the right thing at the right time.

If my joke seems quite ordinary to you, I won't object. I'm not someone who regularly makes quick quips. I'm the kind who goes home and lies awake at night, thinking, "I *should* have told him."

∞

It is no great trick to become a capable craftsman with the tools of speech. With practice anyone can, just as any carpenter can learn how to use a hammer and saw to frame a house. That is my hope for this book: that those who read it will gain such basic competence.

There is something better than mere competence, however. Any woodsman can cut down a tree with his chainsaw, but some can use a chainsaw to carve a statue. That's artistry.

Real artistry with words comes when you learn how to say the right thing at the right time. It may not be anything clever or funny. It may be simply the right word of compassion to someone who is discouraged, or the right word of warning to someone who is headed for trouble. It's the right word at the right *time*.

How can you tell when you've said the right words? You can tell by the fruit they produce. You can tell because your words make a difference. They stick in the mind of those who hear them. Months or even years later, when you've forgotten all about it, those people will thank you. They'll tell you that what you said helped them.

It's not eloquence. You might suppose that to become an artist with words you need a large, fancy vocabulary. Nothing could be further from the truth. People aren't often helped or moved by eloquence. You can eloquently blather away while someone who's attuned to the situation says a few plain words of enduring value.

Popie, for example, once wrote an encouraging note to an older man in our Sunday school class. She genuinely liked and appreciated him, so one day she jotted him a few lines to say how she felt. It was nothing extraordinary, but it arrived at an extraordinary time in his life. He was newly retired, his only daughter was estranged, and he felt the great uncertainties of age coming on. He needed encouragement just then.

"Several times," he told us a year or so later, "when I've been feeling discouraged, I've pulled out that note just to read it again."

Anyone who wants to have this kind of impact can have

it, of course, just by setting out to write notes of encouragement to everyone they know. The scattershot method will certainly bear fruit. Unfortunately, most of us lack the time to do this. Certainly Popie lacks it; she's a very busy woman. She simply can't write notes to everyone she would like to. She is remarkably good, however, at sensing times when people especially need a word of encouragement. She's an artist in that way.

I remember another occasion, under very different circumstances, when she seized the moment. In the church fellowship hall between services. Popie had coffee with a friend whose wife was dying of cancer. Richard is of Scandinavian parentage. Though he is a very passionate man, he is not very good at expressing his feelings. Popie quickly saw that he was finding it extraordinarily difficult to connect with his wife. Carol was sick with chemotherapy and emotionally very up and down. When she began crying, as she often did, Richard didn't know what to say. He felt helpless and stupid.

All this came out in a few minutes over a cup of coffee. What do you say to someone who's obviously struggling? Especially in a crowded church fellowship hall when you only have a few minutes? I know what I typically do. I look glum, I try to show a bit of sympathy, and I get out of there as soon as I can.

Here's what Popie said: "Richard, we only have a few minutes, so I am going to tell you what to do. If you came to my office, I would spend a lot of time listening to you and empathizing with your feelings. But I don't think you're going to come into my office, so I am going to tell you what to do. *Hold her.* You don't have to say anything. Put your arms around her. Let her cry, and hold her."

He later said that was the advice that got him through the months leading up to Carol's death.

∽o∽

Do you have the gift to sense a need and respond to it? It's a talent I'm most familiar with in sports. Great ballplayers manage to be in the right place at the critical time. They anticipate the crucial bounce. They may seem just lucky to be where the ball comes down, but they do it so consistently that you realize it is not luck.

Some people are that way with their words. They may be unimpressive on a daily basis, but at the critical moment they say the right thing, the helpful thing.

How do athletes develop the talent for making the big play?

First, such athletes invariably set high expectations for themselves. They are not content merely to do their part—they want to score. They are determined to make the key play. So they are constantly and keenly looking for the opportunity. They play with controlled aggression, poised and ready to move forcefully at any moment.

Second, they play the game a lot, and they do it seriously, paying careful attention. They think afterwards about what happened. They study the game and begin to see patterns, and then to anticipate patterns. Often they cannot really explain these patterns to you—they just know them and are ready for what comes next.

The same factors apply in conversation. People who say the right thing at the right time are invariably people who care about their words. They care about people too and are determined to help them by what they say. When they encounter someone in need, they aren't content simply to escape the situation without embarrassing themselves. They really want to help, and they are determined to help. They set high expectations for themselves.

And they have paid a great deal of attention to real-life conversations. They think hard about what was said—about what helped, about what did not help, and about what might have helped if someone had thought to say it. They begin to anticipate patterns, and they are ready to respond to the critical moment.

This is an art, not a science. I can't give you formulas. Only your determination and your close attention over a long period of time will teach you.

I can, however, describe some of the patterns you need to know.

∾

Key moments start with greetings and good-byes. Think about it. In the morning, you drag yourself to the kitchen for your first cup of coffee, and there you encounter your son. He might just grunt at you. Or he might say, "Hi, Dad. How did you sleep?" How does that greeting affect your day?

Then you go to the office, and you meet your coworkers. At some workplaces, people are too preoccupied to mumble more than a passing hello. At other workplaces, people seem genuinely glad to see each other. What kind of tone is set in the office in those first few minutes of the day, when people act glad to see you?

Even more crucial, I think, is how you greet your family at the end of the workday. A friend of mine told me once about his usual drive home from the office. As he got nearer, he would feel his spirit rising with the anticipation of seeing his wife and young kids. Filled with snug thoughts of his family, he would park his car in the garage—and before he even opened the door, he would hear his children screaming at each other. All of a sudden, invariably, he felt angry.

If you come in the door and find your spouse cooking in the kitchen, how do you greet him or her? If you do it warmly and caringly, doesn't it set a tone for the rest of the evening? If you act grumpy and impatient, doesn't *that* set a tone for the evening?

Greetings are words we don't usually think about. Certainly, most people wouldn't consider them crucial opportunities to say the right thing. Yet they are very powerful. If you convey interest, concern, and warmth through your greeting, the rest of the conversation will reflect it. Often it's as simple as your tone of voice. When you begin with a smile and your full attention, you welcome the other person into your world. We exchange greetings dozens of times a day, often with the same people, but the way we do it determines a great deal about what happens afterwards.

Parting words are similarly powerful. When you leave people, those last words will stick in their minds. If you give them the sense that you're in a hurry or that you're glad to get away, that impression sticks. If you throw in some final word of unwelcome advice, that last irritation will dominate the whole memory of your time together. (Parents are particularly prone to do this with their children—even though most of us can remember not liking it when our parents did it to us.) On the other hand, a warm and loving farewell can compensate for a mediocre visit. You look her in the eye, you hug her, you say, "Thanks so much for having me. You are a very important person in my life. I love you a lot." That can overshadow everything else as you drive away.

That's why putting your children to bed is such an

important ritual; it's what they think of as they drift off to sleep. It's why kissing your spouse good-bye matters; the kiss lingers on the way to work. When you leave people's bedside in the hospital, when you say good-bye to friends moving away, when you're packing up after a visit to your folks, take care of your parting words.

Sometimes when I'm leaving, I'm so concerned with catching my flight, with my next meeting, with my work, that I "leave" before I've gone out the door. I turn my attention prematurely to the next item on my agenda. My body is still there, but my soul has gone. I need to work at staying fully present, in my words as well as my body language, while I say good-bye.

Tolstoy's novel *Anna Karenina* contains a scene that reminded me of how young lovers say farewell. Levin is going off hunting with two of his friends, who talk as they wait for him outside the house.

> "Well, and what about our host?" [one friend] asked.
> "A young wife," said Stepan Arkadyevich, smiling.
> "Yes, and such a charming one!"
> "He came down dressed. No doubt he's run up to her again."
> Stepan Arkadyevich guessed right. Levin had run up again to his wife to ask her once more if she forgave him for his idiocy yesterday. . . .

Tolstoy, who was so good at capturing ordinary human emotions, knew that good-byes are especially difficult for newly married people—and that this can be amusing to those who have been married for some time. The world would be better, however, if couples never lost their sensitivity to good-byes. Newlyweds know how important it is to leave on the right note, because their minds are fully focused on their spouse. It's only when they stop focusing on their partner that they leave without a proper farewell.

∽∾∽

Prayers and blessings are also key words. They are significant because they bring God into the relationship.

When I put my children to bed, or when we pray together as a family—even when we bury a beloved hamster—I try hard to use meaningful words. That doesn't mean cooking up great emotions or trying to turn bedtime into a revival service. It means thinking about what I'm saying and trying to avoid clichés. It means using the tools of speech well—praising sincerely and talking honestly about troubles. Such prayers and blessings are key words because they bring my whole family into my relationship with God—and God into my relationship with my whole family.

A blessing is a particular kind of prayer. John Trent and Gary Smalley have written well in *The Blessing* about how to bless those you love, as a deliberate strategy for encouraging and strengthening them. You bless a person by asking God to build him up—and you do it in the person's presence. You envision good things that can happen in that person's life, and you stand with God and say, "Let's make it so."

Suppose a friend is going off to face a difficult situation at work. You bless that friend by saying, "May God give you courage to say the right words." That may seem a little too pious if you're not used to blessings. But isn't it better to take the risk? Isn't a blessing potentially better than "Have a nice day"?

I remember when my friends Mike and Lesley moved into their house. Years before, Mike had chosen to teach high school over a more lucrative career in engineering; Lesley had chosen to stay at home with their children. That meant they didn't have a lot of money. At times a house had seemed like an impossible dream. Finally, though, they scrimped together enough money and reached their goal.

We had a house-warming party, and I was asked to lead in prayer. I saw it as a key moment. I prayed something like this:

> Dear Father, you know we have waited a long time for this happy day. We prayed for this day and hoped for this day and sometimes despaired that it would ever come. You know that at times it did not seem possible Mike and Lesley would ever be able to buy a house. You know that they were willing to live in an apartment indefinitely if that was necessary. Thank you for their faithfulness. And thank you so much for giving them this house to live in. Make this a day of rejoicing for them. Bring into their hearts, and all of our hearts, a deep sense of thankfulness, for you are very kind to your children.
>
> And Father, do not let this house get in the way of Mike and Lesley's continued faithfulness to you. Don't let it be an idol to them. Rather, make this house a place of shelter for people in need, a place where your name will be lifted up. Enable Mike and Lesley to carry on your ministry, and to do it even better because you have given them this house. We pray this in the name of Jesus. Amen.

I don't know whether anyone else remembers that prayer or not, but I think I said the right word at the right time, and I think it was a key time. Every time we pray, it's a key time.

∽o∽

Times of transition are key times. The purchase of a first house is a major transition in the life of a family, so the words (or prayers) you offer at that time can make a difference. It's the same with a job change, a move to a new location, or the first day at a new school. When people are in transition, they're vulnerable. Often they're frightened. They're also very alert, thinking a lot. Their patterns of life are being thrown in the air, and they have a chance to act in new ways. When people are in transition, your words can matter more than ever.

That's why it's important to meet new neighbors when they first move into the area. I know I haven't always done very well at this. Often I've told myself that I don't want to bother them while they're so busy moving in. But later on, after they've settled into a new routine, it's much harder to make a connection. People in transition are like newly hatched ducklings—liable to bond with whatever they meet.

Out of all the many transitions of our busy lives three are most important: marrying, burying, and birthing. At these times people are filled with emotions. Their lives are changing dramatically. Of all times, these times require that the right words be said. They are key opportunities.

Oftentimes—especially at funerals—we don't see them as opportunities. At funerals people dread saying the wrong thing, so they may not say anything significant at all. Around weddings or births there's so much activity and excitement that nobody may think to say anything of substance.

But a few people may—and if they're the right people saying the right thing, they'll make a great contribution.

I remember two people who did so at the time of my

wedding. One was my brother. He stopped me and said, "A lot of times people are so busy around their wedding that it all becomes a blur, and afterwards they can't really remember much of it. Try to take time to savor this wonderful thing that is happening." It was a powerful word for me to hear. It made a difference for me.

Another word came from my pastor. Popie and I were having struggles as we went to him for our last counseling session. He knew us both well. He didn't downplay the problems we were having, but he expressed great confidence in us as a couple. "I'm really looking forward to seeing the kind of marriage the two of you create." It was a word of confidence that helped us at that moment and projected a hopeful vision of our future.

At such times of transition, be alert to opportunities to say the important thing, the right thing. Look for the word that helps and heals.

∽0∽

One more key opportunity: when someone is being victimized. A single word of warning or dissent can make a powerful difference when people are ridiculing someone, when they are planning something mean, when they are showing prejudice. It takes courage to speak—but oh, how the words echo.

"I feel like we're gossiping. Can we change the subject?"

"She may be all those things, but she is my friend, and I don't want to talk this way about her."

"You know, it makes me very unhappy to hear that kind of joke."

"Could you leave him alone, please?"

∽∘∽

Certain principles can help you speak effectively at a critical moment:

Be in tune with the emotions of the situation. Usually that means matching joy with joy, grief with grief. If people are celebrating at a wedding, it's not the time for philosophic discourse. If people at a funeral are matter-of-fact in their grieving, you won't communicate with them by wailing and thrashing around. You want to meet them where they are. If their emotions are intense, share that intensity. If they are thinking about facts and details, meet them there. Don't try to reverse their emotions.

Sometimes the grief you see in your friends is just unbearable; you long to bring some encouragement, some silver lining to the clouds. The greatest encouragement, however, is simply to accept their feelings and to empathize with them to the degree you're able. Maybe they're very angry with God. You may not agree with what they say, but you aren't required to argue them into another state of mind. In time they will probably feel different. Today the right word will meet them in their grief.

"My heart is breaking for you."

"I don't know what to say, except that I love you."

"I would give anything to undo what happened."

On the other hand, be careful not to stereotype emotions. People at a wedding aren't always gleeful; sometimes they're frightened, sober, or even glum. And sometimes people at a funeral aren't sad. They may feel impatient, relieved, or even giddy. You have to pick up those feelings, and be in tune with them as much as you can.

Be yourself. The right word at the right time is the one *you're* equipped to give. My wife is able to dive immediately into people's emotions. My style is more cautious. In the final analysis, we have to work within our own personalities. An engineer may never be able to reach all the giddy heights and the depressive lows of other people's emotions. His right word may have more to do with careful analysis and planning. You can't be anybody but yourself, so don't try.

Emphasize kindness. Popie and I tell our kids, "If you don't know what to say, and you don't know what to do, smile. You'll almost always be all right if you smile."

It's a rule that works for adults as well. Sometimes I try too hard to say something brilliant or insightful, something that will powerfully affect the people I care about in their time of need. What people remember most—and need most too—is simple kindness.

"I love you."

"I have been praying for you, and I will keep on praying for you, for I know God cares as much as I do."

"Don't ever forget you mean so much to me."

Understand your role, which is determined by your relationship with the people involved. Are you, because of your deep friendship or family relationship, in a leading role? Or are you part of the chorus? If you're in a leading role, you will need to take initiative. Step up and propose a toast. Say your speech. Your age and position also have something to do with this. If you're older, if you're in a position of authority, or if you have a certain amount of fame—even very local—you will usually need to take a more prominent role. It doesn't matter whether you feel important. The way you're seen obligates you.

But if you belong in the chorus, your role is supportive.

Don't overdo it. It can be very annoying when acquaintances assume a role that's bigger than their friendship. Nobody likes it when an unknown cousin proposes two long toasts at a banquet.

Understand what's been said already, and focus on what still needs to be said. You don't need to repeat. When someone gets a big honor, for example, and you're the twentieth person to congratulate her for it, understand that the glowing commendation you feel in your heart may not need to be expressed. If others have said it at length, you may be better off saying it briefly.

Remember that small is beautiful. People don't even hear long speeches, let alone remember them. At emotional moments they usually can't concentrate for more than a minute. It's helpful to boil your message down to one sentence, one phrase, one word. "Toothbrush," my wife says to our children, and they hear her better than if she says, "I want you to remember to brush your teeth." Often when we're trying to say something significant, we say too much.

Stay out of arguments. There's a time and a place for arguing for your convictions. But most arguments are a waste of time. People usually don't listen to each other when they argue, and they often end up saying words they regret. Your opportunity to say the apt word will diminish as you spend time disputing issues.

It's amazing how often key moments—births, deaths, weddings—produce arguments. I recall the days leading up to my own wedding. There was so much tension! We were trying to produce a celebration that all our friends would remember forever, and naturally we felt the strain! We made mountains out of many molehills.

Small issues seem more significant than they really are

when people are emotionally stressed. So it's a good idea to avoid arguments at births, weddings, funerals, and other emotional occasions. Later on, when things calm down, you can fight if you have to. Generally, you don't have to. Ninety-nine percent of all arguments are pointless.

CHAPTER EIGHT

The Power of Words

"Who gave man his mouth? Who makes him deaf or mute?
Who gives him sight or makes him blind? Is it not I, the Lord?
Now go; I will help you speak and will teach you what to say."

(Exodus 4:11–12)

⊰∘⊱

I began this book with a series of pictures—memories of words that have been powerful in my own and in other people's lives. A hand-knit sweater is worn just once because of a cutting comment. A quiet girl becomes convinced she's a dog through someone's joke at a party. An out-of-work father hears encouragement from a friend. We have all felt the power of words like that—in someone's careless remark, in someone's encouragement, in someone's wisdom.

Most of this book has dealt with practical matters: what to say, when to say it. The power of words is more than that, however. Words can change the very core of your being and point your life in a new direction. For words and heart walk closely together.

Jesus said we will be judged by our words: "For out of the overflow of the heart the mouth speaks. The good man brings good things out of the good stored up in him, and the evil man brings evil things out of the evil stored up in him. But I tell you that men will have to give account on the day of judgment for every careless word they have spoken. For by your words you will be acquitted, and by your words you will be condemned" (Matthew 12:34–37).

A person can be condemned simply for careless words? Jesus could say this because he knew that our words reveal our true selves. Speech is never truly accidental. If you listen to someone talk long enough, you will know what kind of person he or she is. Our careless words may reveal more than our carefully planned speeches. We open up our mouth, and out pops our heart.

If you have ever tried to change your way of talking, you've realized this. Just try, for example, to eliminate harsh words. That doesn't sound so difficult. But you'll find them cropping up in the most unruly way. They'll rush out of your mouth without warning. Through the effort you'll discover how much meanness is in your heart, for it keeps bubbling up. You'll have to face not just your careless words but yourself.

Or try to begin honestly praising someone. Why won't the words come out? Why is it such an effort simply to say, "I love you" or "Your friendship is very important to me" or "I really appreciated your work"? The reason can only be that at heart you are not an admiring and a giving person. To change your words, you must change your heart as well. That requires prayer, meditation, the help of loved ones, and above all, the help of God.

Changing your speech isn't superficial. It's not "acting nice" or "trying to sound good." It goes to the heart. Your talk is a rudder by which you can steer your life.

∽

There's another point of view on this, very commonly held today. It sees words not as tools for transformation but as tools for self-expression. In this view, you are what you are, and your job is to express that. Words are something like steam whistles, vents that must be opened to let out hot and turbulent feelings. Someone says horrible things to another person and justifies it by saying, "That's just the way I feel." Apparently, anything you feel, you can say—or *should* say.

In my college dormitory lived a faculty resident known fondly as Doc. Doc was an engineering professor whose life had been transformed by the Esalen Institute, a place near Big Sur, California, where encounter groups were developed in the sixties. Doc took to wearing beads and organizing encounter groups in the dorm.

In encounter groups people were encouraged to throw caution to the wind and express anything and everything. They were supposed to get in touch with their true feelings. If they wept, moaned, and screamed, that was good. Doc believed completely in these encounter groups. He believed that any problem could be solved through expressing your feelings.

Doc's experiments ran into problems when one of the two dorms he supervised became a Chicano theme house. This was a dorm with activities oriented toward a Mexican-American theme. It attracted—as it was meant to—students who had grown up in tough Hispanic neighborhoods. Some students from East Los Angeles had different ideas, for example, about what time of the night a person should turn down his stereo. When one student knocked on another's door to tell him to turn it down, it started a fist fight. A series of incidents showed that getting along together was not going to be easy.

Doc saw this as the ideal setting for encounter-group tactics. He organized meetings where he encouraged students to express their feelings as freely as possible. Those from the barrio generally found this easy to do. They used quite colorful language to describe their emotions. Doc was pleased. Finally he had found students who were in touch with their inner selves! They held nothing back! The trouble was that self-expression didn't solve the problems. The feelings tended to spiral out of control. Eventually, after several long, pointless shouting matches, the encounter groups were abandoned.

Doc's assumption—the assumption of the sixties—was that people are all right at heart. Nothing needs transforming; it just needs expressing. The problem is repression and artificiality.

In reality, however, when we have done away with all artificiality, we are left with a far more fundamental difficulty: ourselves. We are not loving, wise, and caring people at heart. All too often we are self-seeking, uncaring prima donnas. We need to be transformed. Our words and our hearts need transforming.

I think of a woman who was greatly influenced (and helped) by counseling. Through most of her life she had repressed her anger. For a short time she was deeply depressed and unable to work. Therapy helped her to become aware of her feelings and to break out of the depression.

Now when she's angry or anxious, it all spills out. That's good, to a point. She's a little confused, though, as to why the feelings don't get better. After years of spilling her guts, she's as angry and anxious as ever—perhaps more so. The reason, I think, is that she has understood words as tools of self-expression, not as tools of transformation. She hasn't learned to express those feelings in a way that's constructive and healing. She hasn't learned how to wisely talk about trouble—she just "bombs away." She hasn't let her words reveal to her the conflicts in herself that she must resolve. She hasn't seen that she must work through her words—and God's—toward healing.

∽∾

Consider the Adams family of Eden. The parents got arrested for a petty burglary. They were evicted from the farm. The oldest boy killed his brother. The family—aunts and uncles and cousins and all—lost everything in a big flood. They rebuilt, but when they were putting together a large development project, they quarreled and couldn't speak to each other. The building was never completed. Now the family has split into various clans that are constantly fighting.

How would you help such a family? If you had all the resources in the world, how would you reach them? What would be powerful enough to transform them?

The Adams family is the human family, described in the first eleven chapters of Genesis. God made this family and then watched them try to destroy themselves. "The Lord was grieved that he had made man on the earth, and his heart was filled with pain" (Genesis 6:6).

Yet God is determined to redeem the family he has made. How does he do it? He speaks to them. Every time God wants the attention of the human race, he talks. Often they don't listen. Sometimes a few do. Yet he sticks to words. His followers revere a book that records his words. They understand them to be words that give life.

That is the power of words. It is not *just* words, of course, for God ultimately gave himself. Transformation began, however, with God speaking.

So it will be with us. To transform our own hearts and the hearts of others, we must follow God's strategy. We must hear the words of God himself speaking to us, and we must speak them to others.

From the Beginning, God Made Promises

God appeared to Abraham and said, "I will bless you." He projected a future beyond anything that Abraham could imagine. With Noah, with David, with prophets like Isaiah, he made promises in a similar manner.

If we are to join in his transforming project, we must also speak promisingly. We need to lift sights above the here and now to envision a great future. Above all, that future will be the one that God promises his people. We need to talk about the kingdom of heaven. We need to speak of a time when we will live with Jesus.

It's unfashionable to talk this way. We prefer to concentrate on blessings we can expect this week—emotional, spiritual, and financial blessings. Yet God's promises are seldom fulfilled overnight. As the book of Hebrews says, God's people "were still living by faith when they died. They did not receive the things promised; they only saw them and welcomed them from a distance" (Hebrews 11:13). It was their vision of a good future, nevertheless, that transformed their lives in the here and now.

I find it easy to lose a sense of God's promise in my conversation. With my children I talk about their schoolwork, their manners, their friends—but I seldom manage to bring these into the perspective of God's coming kingdom. I need to—not only for their good but for my own. As my words bend toward the future that God intends for me and for them, my life becomes more alert to his kingdom, less obsessed with my own short-term gains and losses. That's transformation.

God's Words Challenge

When you read the Bible, you find many promises and

much encouragement, but you also find demands. Read what Jesus had to say. His words cut to the heart of his disciples. He expected commitment. He demanded holiness. He called them to be "perfect, therefore, as your heavenly Father is perfect" (Matthew 5:48).

If we are to talk like God, we will challenge. This is unfashionable too. It's easier to embrace an all-purpose tolerance that stands for nothing, opposes nothing. But if we talk like God, people will know what is right and what is wrong. They will see the gap between what they are and what they should be. Mediocrity will be challenged to a higher standard. Laziness will be challenged to hard work. Apathy will be challenged to commitment. Selfishness will be challenged to service. Prejudice will be challenged to love. Immorality will be challenged to righteousness.

As we speak such words with love, we will not be able to ignore our own behavior. We too will be challenged—and transformed.

God's Words Are Always Loving

The Bible includes some hard assessments and some candid words, but overall, what kind of message does it give overall? Always, its message is of love and hope. "Ever since I heard about your faith in the Lord Jesus . . . I have not stopped giving thanks for you, remembering you in my prayers" (Ephesians 1:15–16). "In all my prayers for all of you, I always pray with joy . . . being confident of this, that he who began a good work in you will carry it on to completion" (Philippians 1:4–6).

Those are the apostle Paul's words of encouragement to two of the early churches, and they are typical of God's Spirit at work in words. Paul never flattered. He could—and did—tell the hard truth. He confronted problems. Yet he wrote lovingly, so that people knew how precious they were to God and to Paul.

The words of the Bible—some directly spoken by God, some from people filled with his Spirit—use poetry, history, sermons, personal letters, census reports. There is a style to suit every mood and every occasion. However, in every style, you can discover the God who is love.

To speak of God's love—and to speak *with* God's love—matters more than all the wise advice or eloquent encouragement I can muster. It goes beyond affirmation and apt words and skillful confrontation. I know this because I have experienced it. My parents have given me many good words over my life. Nothing they said has been so transforming, however, as the message that God is love. I saw (and heard) that they experienced this love for themselves. I learned about its importance for me. I want that same love to affect and infect everything I say. I want to speak like God—full of love—and in so doing develop a character more like his, which is loving. That is transformation.

Appendix:
Selected Scriptures on Words*

The creative power of words shows in God's creation of the universe. By speaking, he creates. God's speech does not merely comment on reality, it creates reality. So throughout the Bible, God's word is active and powerful in transforming the world.

> In the beginning God created the heavens and the earth. . . . And God said, "Let there be light," and there was light. . . . (Genesis 1:1,3)

God's help. When God called Moses to lead his people out of Egypt, Moses objected that he was not a good talker. But God said natural talent was no limitation. He would teach Moses how to talk.

So it is today when some people say they can't change the way they speak—they're just not good at giving compliments, or expressing their feelings. Natural talent isn't the real problem. The difficulty is in willingness to learn.

> Moses said to the Lord, "O Lord, I have never been eloquent, neither in the past nor since you have spoken to your servant. I am slow of speech and tongue."
> The Lord said to him, "Who gave man his mouth? Who makes him deaf or mute? Who gives him sight or

---

* All Scriptures are indented. A brief commentary precedes them, with key words highlighted in bold text. You can flip through this appendix looking for the subjects that particularly interest you.

makes him blind? Is it not I, the Lord? Now go; I will help you speak and will teach you what to say" (Exodus 4:10–12).

The basic requirement. One of the Ten Fundamentals of law (The Ten Commandments) is God's requirement that no one lie in a way that will hurt his neighbor. God requires more of our speech, of course, but his requirements start here.

You shall not give false testimony against your neighbor. (Exodus 20:16)

Word and heart. This deep prayer links our words to our heart—and perceives that both are crucial to a life that pleases God.

May the words of my mouth and the meditation of my heart be pleasing in your sight, O Lord, my Rock and my Redeemer. (Psalm 19:14)

Speech as an investment. Speaking well is as much an investment in the future as planting seeds in springtime, or going to work in the morning.

From the fruit of his lips a man is filled with good things as surely as the work of his hands rewards him. (Proverbs 12:14)

From the fruit of his mouth a man's stomach is filled; with the harvest from his lips he is satisfied.
The tongue has the power of life and death, and those who love it will eat its fruit. (Proverbs 18:20,21)

Deceitful words. While our words should be encouraging and affirming, they should never be duplicitous.

Like a coating of glaze over earthenware
are fervent lips with an evil heart.
A malicious man disguises himself with his lips,
but in his heart he harbors deceit.
Though his speech is charming, do not believe him,
for seven abominations fill his heart. (Proverbs 26:23–25)

The tongue that brings healing is a tree of life,
but a deceitful tongue crushes the spirit. (Proverbs 15:4)

Encouraging words can change another person's out-
look just when he is most weighed down. They don't just
cheer up someone's day, they penetrate to the bone.

An anxious heart weighs a man down,
but a kind word cheers him up. (Proverbs 12:25)

Pleasant words are a honeycomb,
sweet to the soul and healing to the bones. (Proverbs
16:24)

Thoughtful and careful words. Speaking well and
wisely takes a great deal of care. Tremendous harm is done
by speaking without thinking.

Do you see a man who speaks in haste?
There is more hope for a fool than for him. (Proverbs
29:20)

The heart of the righteous weighs its answers,
but the mouth of the wicked gushes evil. (Proverbs
15:28)

Reckless words pierce like a sword,
but the tongue of the wise brings healing. (Proverbs
12:18)

Keeping your mouth shut. Sometimes the greatest sign of wisdom is silence.

When words are many, sin is not absent,
but he who holds his tongue is wise. (Proverbs 10:19)

A prudent man keeps his knowledge to himself,
but the heart of fools blurts out folly. (Proverbs 12:23)

Even a fool is thought wise if he keeps silent,
and discerning if he holds his tongue. (Proverbs 17:28)

He who answers before listening—
that is his folly and his shame. (Proverbs 18:13)

Speaking up for others. Sometimes, however, it is a sin to remain silent.

Speak up for those who cannot speak for themselves,
for the rights of all who are destitute.
Speak up and judge fairly;
defend the rights of the poor and needy. (Proverbs 31:8–9)

Soft words. When you're talking about trouble, try to turn down the cycle of anger, instead of feeding into it. There's a special power in gentleness.

A gentle answer turns away wrath,
but a harsh word stirs up anger. (Proverbs 15:1)

Through patience a ruler can be persuaded,
and a gentle tongue can break a bone. (Proverbs 25:15)

Boasting is inappropriate behavior.

Let another praise you, and not your own mouth;
someone else, and not your own lips. (Proverbs 27:2)

Lies are detestable to God.

The Lord detests lying lips,
but he delights in men who are truthful. (Proverbs 12:22)

A false witness will not go unpunished,
and he who pours out lies will perish. (Proverbs 19:9)

Flattery is more than false. It's fundamentally hostile,
setting a person up for his downfall.

A lying tongue hates those it hurts,
and a flattering mouth works ruin. (Proverbs 26:28)

Whoever flatters his neighbor
is spreading a net for his feet. (Proverbs 29:5)

Gossip destroys friendships, betrays confidences, and
feeds quarrels.

A gossip betrays a confidence,
but a trustworthy man keeps a secret. (Proverbs 11:13)

A perverse man stirs up dissension,
and a gossip separates close friends. (Proverbs 16:28)

He who covers over an offense promotes love,
but whoever repeats the matter separates close friends.
(Proverbs 17:9)

The words of a gossip are like choice morsels;
they go down to a man's inmost parts. (Proverbs 18:8)

Without wood a fire goes out;
without gossip a quarrel dies down. (Proverbs 26:20)

Consider the person. You must tailor your words to the
person you're speaking to. Especially in dealing with trouble,

you must consider in advance whether he or she is willing
and able to accept rebuke.

Do not answer a fool according to his folly,
or you will be like him yourself. (Proverbs 26:4)

Do not speak to a fool,
for he will scorn the wisdom of your words. (Proverbs
23:9)

Whoever corrects a mocker invites insult;
whoever rebukes a wicked man incurs abuse.
Do not rebuke a mocker or he will hate you;
rebuke a wise man and he will love you.
Instruct a wise man and he will be wiser still;
teach a righteous man and he will add to his learning.
(Proverbs 9:7–9)

Talking about trouble is difficult, but may be "life-giving." It's a sign of wisdom to listen to others' correction. It's
a sign of friendship to give correction.

Better is open rebuke
than hidden love.
Wounds from a friend can be trusted,
but an enemy multiplies kisses. (Proverbs 27:5,6)

He who rebukes a man will in the end gain more favor
than he who has a flattering tongue. (Proverbs 28:23)

He who listens to a life-giving rebuke
will be at home among the wise. (Proverbs 15:31)

As iron sharpens iron,
so one man sharpens another. (Proverbs 27:17)

Perfume and incense bring joy to the heart,
and the pleasantness of one's friend springs from his
earnest counsel. (Proverbs 27:9)

Saying the right thing at the right time requires more
than cleverness. It is an aspect of righteousness. Only those
with a pure heart will consistently know the right thing to
say.

The lips of the righteous know what is fitting,
but the mouth of the wicked only what is perverse.
(Proverbs 10:32)

The art of timing. There's an art to saying the right
thing at the right time. (And there's a mess when your timing is off.) The right response is as beautiful as a piece of
well-made jewelry.

A man finds joy in giving an apt reply—
and how good is a timely word! (Proverbs 15:23)

If a man loudly blesses his neighbor early in the morning,
it will be taken as a curse. (Proverbs 27:14)

Like one who takes away a garment on a cold day,
or like vinegar poured on soda,
is one who sings songs to a heavy heart. (Proverbs 25:20)

A word aptly spoken
is like apples of gold in settings of silver. (Proverbs 25:11)

Angry words, Jesus emphasized, have murderous impli-
cations. After hearing Jesus' words talk on this, could anyone say in self-defense, "I was just talking"?

You have heard that it was said to the people long ago,

"Do not murder, and anyone who murders will be subject
to judgment." But I tell you that . . .Anyone who says,
"You fool!" will be in danger of the fire of hell. (Matthew
5:21–22)

Oaths are necessary only when people have developed
the habit of telling little white lies. Jesus, however, said simple truthtelling was all that was needed.

You have heard that it was said to the people long ago,
"Do not break your oath. . . ." But I tell you, Do not swear
at all. . . . Simply let your "Yes" be "Yes" and your "No,"
"No." Anything beyond this comes from the evil one.
(Matthew 5:33–37)

Hypocritical words. Jesus was well aware that people's
words can be hypocritical. He warned that their words must
be matched by their behavior.

Not everyone who says to me, "Lord, Lord," will enter
the kingdom of heaven, but only he who does the will of
my Father who is in heaven. (Matthew 7:21)

Judged by our words. Nevertheless, Jesus regarded our
words as part of the fruit that our lives produce. We can and
will be judged by the words we have said—including the
careless words.

The good man brings good things out of the good stored
up in him, and the evil man brings evil things out of the
evil stored up in him. But I tell you that men will have to
give account on the day of judgment for every careless
word they have spoken. For by your words you will be
acquitted, and by your words you will be condemned.
(Matthew 12:35–37)

God's best word to us. Jesus, someone has said, was all

that God wanted to say to us. John calls Jesus the Word, God's eternally creative communication.

> In the beginning was the Word, and the Word was with God, and the Word was God. . . . The Word became flesh and made his dwelling among us. (John 1:1,14)

Words and heart. Our response to Jesus must be in both our words and our hearts. As everywhere in Scripture, the two are tied together.

> If you confess with your mouth, "Jesus is Lord," and believe in your heart that God raised him from the dead, you will be saved. (Romans 10:9)

Words of blessing. Our words should be consistently positive, regardless of the way others treat us. We should tune our words to the emotions of the person to whom we're speaking.

> Bless those who persecute you; bless and do not curse. Rejoice with those who rejoice; mourn with those who mourn. (Romans 12:14,15)

The simple truth, with love. Communicating truth and love is far more important than speaking with eloquence and feeling.

> When I came to you, brothers, I did not come with eloquence or superior wisdom. . . My message and my preaching were not with wise and persuasive words, but with a demonstration of the Spirit's power. (1 Corinthians 2:1,4)

> If I speak in the tongues of men and of angels, but have not love, I am only a resounding gong or a clanging cymbal. (1 Corinthians 13:1)

If anyone speaks, he should do it as one speaking the very words of God. (1 Peter 4:11)

Serving others with our words. Among Christians, everyday talk should be calculated to build others up. Our own self-expression or amusement come a distant second to that goal.

In the church I would rather speak five intelligible words to instruct others than ten thousand words in a tongue. (1 Corinthians 14:19)

Therefore each of you must put off falsehood and speak truthfully to his neighbor, for we are all members of one body. . . . Do not let any unwholesome talk come out of your mouths, but only what is helpful for building others up according to their needs. . . .Nor should there be obscenity, foolish talk or coarse joking, which are out of place, but rather thanksgiving. . . . Speak to one another with psalms, hymns and spiritual songs. (Ephesians 4:25, 29; 5:4, 19)

The tongue is a rudder. James emphasizes that a well-controlled tongue is a fundamental aspect of righteousness. He also introduces the idea that the tongue should be a kind of rudder steering our lives. More often, though, it is like a spark in a dry forest. We no more "tame" the tongue than we eliminate sin from our lives. As with fire, as with poison, we must always be watchful.

My dear brothers, take note of this: Everyone should be quick to listen, slow to speak and slow to become angry, for man's anger does not bring about the righteous life that God desires. . . . If anyone considers himself religious and yet does not keep a tight rein on his tongue, he deceives himself and his religion is worthless. (James 1:19, 20, 26)

We all stumble in many ways. If anyone is never at fault in what he says, he is a perfect man, able to keep his whole body in check.

When we put bits into the mouths of horses to make them obey us, we can turn the whole animal. Or take ships as an example. Although they are so large and are driven by strong winds, they are steered by a very small rudder wherever the pilot wants to go. Likewise the tongue is a small part of the body, but it makes great boasts. Consider what a great forest is set on fire by a small spark. The tongue also is a fire, a world of evil among the parts of the body. It corrupts the whole person, sets the whole course of his life on fire, and is itself set on fire by hell.

All kinds of animals, birds, reptiles and creatures of the sea are being tamed and have been tamed by man, but no man can tame the tongue. It is a restless evil, full of deadly poison.

With the tongue we praise our Lord and Father, and with it we curse men, who have been made in God's likeness. Out of the same mouth come praise and cursing. My brothers, this should not be! (James 3:1–10)